PANSHANGER
AERODROME

PANSHANGER AERODROME

MICHAEL PACKHAM

TEMPUS

First published 2006

Tempus Publishing Limited
The Mill, Brimscombe Port,
Stroud, Gloucestershire, GL5 2QG
www.tempus-publishing.com

British Library Cataloguing in Publication Data.
A catalogue record for this book is available from the British Library.

ISBN 0 7524 3917 0
 978 0 7524 3917 4

Typesetting and origination by Tempus Publishing Limited
Printed in Great Britain

Contents

Introduction

From a parcel of land acquired for the war effort, through hectic years of military pilot and apprentice training and civilian private flying, Panshanger Aerodrome has been part of the local landscape. Its contribution to the defence of the country, the opportunities given to train apprentices and offer flying tuition to all is not easily quantified. The ravages of time have taken their toll of the buildings and Panshanger has only partially escaped neglect, modification, the inexorable march of housing development and, sadly, wanton vandalism. Where wartime hangars, accommodation and office blocks once stood, these changes have reduced to rubble, some of necessity but much by needless destruction. There is no doubt that these comments are echoed across the land with the loss of many old wartime aerodromes and it is fortunate for the enthusiast and archaeologist that Panshanger still survives as an active aerodrome, where others, sadly, have disappeared.

My earliest memory of Panshanger Aerodrome is not too distant; in early 1963 at the tender age of six years, I recall travelling with my father in the company van to attend to the 'outer marker' beacon, located in a corner of the airfield. De Havilland paid rent to the aerodrome owner for this facility. As we drove around the perimeter track on the north site we passed the Vickers Viking G-AHPB, stored in the open, and, casting an eye to the other side of the field, saw the huge shape (to me) of the four-engine Canadair C-4, stored the same. My memory became one of a local airport, not an airfield, with an array of yellow and red blister hangars and huts aplenty.

In 1967, whilst I was still at a local JMI school, my family moved to a new house near to the aerodrome on what was then known as the 'Panshanger 1' housing development. Within a few days I saw an aircraft passing very low overhead, a Thruxton Jackaroo G-APAL, landing at the aerodrome, and from then on I was hooked on flying. My first flight was made from the airfield a few months later, June 1967, in Piper Cherokee G-ASEJ. It was just two circuits but enough to convince me this is what I wanted to do for a living – so easily influenced at the tender age of eleven years!

Visiting the airfield was always an adventure. A group arriving on push-bikes armed with note pads was often a red rag to the likes of resident engineers Harry Fenner and Ernie Chick, and we were sent swiftly on our way. On good days and with the appropriate nod from the 'Baron' Derek de Sarigny, we were allowed a lot more freedom. If only a camera had been a regular part of the inventory.

Through a family friend, Paul Newby, I flew in an Auster J-1, G-AGVN, and in March 1968, the highlight of my life, I flew in a Tiger Moth G-ANSP, all from the aerodrome. There

Aerial shot showing the south site, taken on 11 July 1947. (BAE SYSTEMS)

An aerial view taken in June 1996 looks north-east over the aerodrome, showing the ultimate extent of the housing estate. (Author)

were notable weekends when 'Breakfast Patrols' would cause all manner of visitors to attempt to land without being 'spotted' by the resident club aircraft; if you managed, a free breakfast would come your way. I recall a Tiger Moth G-ALBD crawling in to land coming down the street just above tree height.

During the early part of 1970 the aerodrome reopened for flying training and the arrival of three Cessna 150s and a Rollason Condor from Leavesden was encouraging. Typically for Panshanger Aerodrome during this time, the new operation lasted barely a year and a lengthy period in the doldrums followed with the inevitable housing encroaching onto the site. The airfield became notorious for the illegal smuggling of immigrants and other operations, and notably in 1971 the police foiled one such mission, reported with much fanfare in the *Welwyn Hatfield Times*.

The north side of the aerodrome was a haven for surplus aircraft parts and memorabilia, leftovers from the London Aeroplane Club, the Reserve Flying School and Keegan Aviation occupation of the hangars and huts. As there was fortunately little decay of the buildings in the late 1960s, we could find parts for Proctor, Anson, Hornet Moth and Tiger Moth and (rumour had it) parts for Mosquito as well. In 1970, the fuselage and wings of Miles Messenger, G-AJYZ, were left to rot beside one of the north site hangars before being burned.

Through the 1970s Panshanger Aerodrome was a backdrop for several films. During the spring of 1972 the sight of a Bristol Superfreighter lumbering into the air over our house was never to be forgotten and all for the climax of a forgettable comedy film, titled *Rentadick*. Also in 1972 the aerodrome was given a makeover to resemble a German airstrip for *Our Miss Fred*, a film starring Danny La Rue, and a scale replica of a Spanish-built Messerschmitt 109 (ask the producers why) sat on the grass for a while.

Since those days I flew many more times from the aerodrome and learned to fly there from 1976, having transferred from Luton Flying Club with my instructor, Ed James. Panshanger was then almost deserted, without a CAA licence to operate training and in danger of housing swamping the site, although back then the aerodrome was relatively intact. We had to train at Leavesden, having dual cross-country before commencing circuit training. On lucky days at the weekend we used Hatfield, with air traffic and radar, all for free, thanks to British Aerospace.

Through the operations in the 1980s the airfield was fully occupied with flying training, local owners and helicopter operations, and living away from the area my visits were too few to mention other than flights to and from. My father, then working for Air Traffic at British Aerospace, recalled setting up a control building to link between Panshanger and Hatfield with the aim of monitoring circuit traffic with the increased activity in business jets at Hatfield. This was a requirement since business jet pilots were unfamiliar with the aerodrome and its proximity to Hatfield would create potential 'near miss' situations. It seems a long time ago that all this ended in 1992, following the closure of Hatfield and Panshanger.

Coming back to Panshanger in 1992 showed just how much destruction had been wrought in such a brief period following the aerodrome closure, due mainly to a vandalism and the incursion of travellers. Once cleared and the aerodrome secured, the true destruction of the historic buildings and hangars could be seen. During 1993 I purposefully recorded everything on camera. For ten years following reopening, the aerodrome had a fairly relaxed atmosphere with interesting visiting aircraft but the fallout after 9/11 generated increased security and insurance premiums and former paths assumed for public access have been 'stopped up' to prevent incursions. Against all the odds, with the likes of Hatfield (the parent) now under a massive industrial and housing complex, Leavesden (the same) and Radlett (now a large hole in the landscape) all gone, the aerodrome remains active, sitting precariously on the eastern edge of the Panshanger housing estate. Like Elstree, it suffers complaints about noise pollution but also from rumours of impending gravel extraction and erroneous whinging from the general lack of 'air-mindedness' prevailing today.

Mike Packham
April 2006

1

Location and Brief History

Panshanger Aerodrome is situated 3½ miles west of Hertford at Map Reference TL 266128 (O.S.166) and L715323 on the Air Ministry map (No.96). Grid position is 51°48'04"N 00°09'45"W and the aerodrome elevation is 250' ASL. Current runway direction is 290°/110°. Panshanger carried the ICAO (International Civil Aviation Organisation) location code EGLG and IATA (International Airline Transport Association) location P43. Currently the runway directions are 110°/290° with TORA 11 (Take Off Run Available) 857m and LDA 11 (Landing Distance Available) 888m, TORA 29,948m and LDA 29,788m. The differences are a result of starter runway extensions. VHF radio allocation is 120.25 MHz.

The land currently occupied by the aerodrome is a much-reduced portion of the original 248 acres of agricultural land farmed as part of the Panshanger estate (Baron Grenfell and Lady Desborough). By June 1940, under the terms of the Emergency Powers Act (1939), the land was released from the tenant farmers to the Air Ministry. In turn the Air Ministry gave the local aircraft manufacturing concern, de Havilland at Hatfield, authority and responsibility to construct a dummy aircraft works to divert enemy bombers from their facility at Hatfield, some 6 miles to the south.

The decoy factory was constructed from late summer in 1940 and was used from November that year. De Havilland used the fields around the factory as an all-grass Reserve Landing Ground (RLG) for flying training from winter 1940–41 onwards. It was named Holwell Hyde.

The first party of 1 Elementary Flying Training School (1 EFTS) personnel and 8 Tiger Moths moved from Hatfield to Holwell Hyde RLG during the summer of 1941, occupying buildings and hangars erected on the north side of the site. By autumn 1942 more Tigers arrived and further expansion during 1943 continued after the completion of administration, training, fuel and hangarage on a new site in the south-east corner. 1 EFTS was responsible for training Army and Air Force pilots.

The aerodrome was renamed RAF Panshanger in September 1943 and continued in operation for the remainder of the war.

Post-war training was supervised by de Havilland on the north site via the London Aeroplane Club (civilian flying) and the south by reservists of 1 Reserve Flying School (1 RFS), flying at weekends in Tiger Moth, Anson and, from 1950, Chipmunk aircraft. As the headquarters of the county Air Training Corps, a gliding school occupied part of the aerodrome until the early 1950s.

The Reserve School closed in 1953 and civilian flying took over the facility, following the sale of the land into private hands. Periods of activity and lulls into disuse followed but the aerodrome remained a training facility (despite the inevitable intrusion of housing) until its closure in 1992. It re-opened a year later with a new licence to continue as a centre for pilot training. At the time of writing Panshanger is one of only two licensed aerodromes in Hertfordshire.

Ordnance Survey 1:25000 plan from 1956 showing the original aerodrome plan and distinct lack of housing. (Ordnance Survey Crown Copyright)

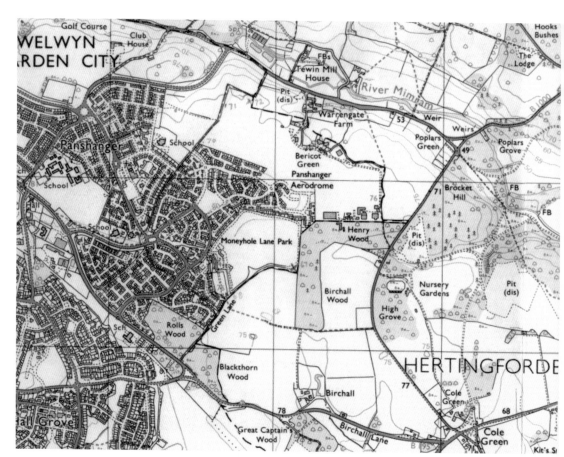

Current Ordnance Survey 1:25000 showing the extent of housing onto the much-reduced aerodrome. (Ordnance Survey Crown Copyright)

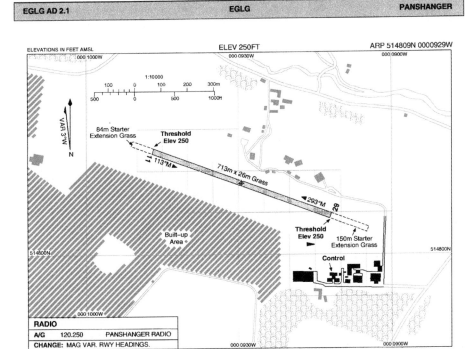

| EGLG AD 2.1 | EGLG | PANSHANGER |

ELEVATIONS IN FEET AMSL

ELEV 250FT

ARP 514809N 0000929W

1:10000

84m Starter
Extension Grass

Threshold
Elev 250

113°M

713m x 26m Grass

293°M

29

VAR 3°W

N

Built-up
Area

Threshold
Elev 250

150m Starter
Extension Grass

Control

514800N

514800N

RADIO		
A/G	120.250	PANSHANGER RADIO
CHANGE: MAG VAR. RWY HEADINGS.		

The aerodrome plan from September 2000. (East Herts Flying School)

Moneyhole Lane Park was the site for the decoy factory and this shot, from June 1996, shows the relatively unspoilt site, isolated by housing. The landscaping of the corner of Birchall Wood was carried out in 1943 to provide better visibility of the whole aerodrome from the newly completed south site. (Author)

2

The Decoy Factory

The land under lease by the Air Ministry was administered by the de Havilland Aircraft Co. and the decoy facility built with them in mind, on the south of the site, from July 1940. The factory was built on the triangle of land at the meeting of Moneyhole Lane and Green Lane, roughly in the position now occupied by the present Moneyhole Lane Park. This area was chosen because of its proximity to Hatfield Aerodrome and an existing railway link, the LNER Hatfield–Hertford branch line, running just to the south of Green Lane, where a station halt named Cole Green had been built. Green Lane provided access, exiting between Rolls Wood and Blackthorn Wood. The site was reasonably remote from local housing and other industrial concerns and made the best use of the available plot for future aerodrome requirements.

The decoy facility was completed by autumn 1940 and classified by the Air Ministry as a 'Works No.M3' (Manufacturing site 3) and later a 'QF/QL' site (QF No.225). Air Ministry papers give the grid position as L715323 (Map 96) and this equates to TL 270128 on the Ordnance Survey Landranger 166 map.

COLONEL JOHN TURNER

Holwell Hyde was selected for use as a daytime decoy aerodrome to divert potential attack on the de Havilland Aircraft Co. facilities at Hatfield, a few miles to the south.

A month after the start of the Second World War, Army Colonel John Turner, controller of deception and camouflage studies at RAF Station Hook, Surbiton, studied possible sites for decoy potential. There was a great desire to protect strategic targets from enemy attack, particularly aerodromes and manufacturing facilities. Initially Turner designed a daytime decoy facility, the so-called 'K' site, which needed to represent an active aerodrome, complete with full-size decoy aircraft suitably positioned to simulate an operational aerodrome during daylight hours. A typical 'K' site was a dummy landing ground with a grassed area at least 700 yards x 40 yards. There were no hangars provided (initially) but petrol and bomb dumps, tracks, paths, trenches, road entrances, windsock, smudge fire, shelters and real machine-gun posts had to be constructed. At least two sunken machine-gun posts, roughly described as enlarged one-man dustbins, were dug up in recent years indicating the extent of the subterfuge, though in consequence these would serve the later aerodrome security too. There is no evidence that Holwell Hyde was selected to be just a 'K' site.

An aerial shot of the decoy facility from late 1941 looks to the south and shows the complete site with decoy Spitfire, Hurricane, Defiant and a Blenheim dispersed around it. Two-dimensional decoys are visible and all 'roads' are painted on the grass. Decoy facility personnel were tented to the south with the access road to what is now Blackfan Road visible to the top of the shot. At least one temporary blast shelter was placed in the woods out of shot to the left. (BAE SYSTEMS)

'M3' AND DECOYS

The land at Holwell Hyde (Panshanger) was selected for its geology: its proximity to de Havilland's production site at Hatfield and the industrial area of Welwyn Garden City. The area was levelled from June 1940 and construction completed by the autumn of that year. Turner's men from Sound City Film Studios at Shepperton, Middlesex, carried out design and construction of the dummy factory facility at Holwell Hyde (Air Ministry Works No.M3).

Holwell Hyde was one of four manufacturing or miscellaneous sites (the 'M' sites), built a few miles from the real thing to represent fully functioning aircraft production facilities. Others were built at Chatham (to protect Short Bros site on the river Medway at Rochester), Coven (for Boulton & Paul at Wolverhampton) and Leamington Hastings (for Armstrong Whitworth at Coventry). Two more decoy facilities were built to protect Air Ministry wireless telegraphy stations, these being at Leighton Buzzard and Dagnall. All were completed by the end of summer 1940.

There were strict rules to the construction of the sites; Holwell Hyde appeared no different. No site could be less than 400 yards from occupied houses and not less than 800 yards from a village or 1 mile from a town, therefore it was preferable to use open countryside. Dugouts were to be provided if anybody was within 800 yards of the site. By 12 September 1940 an extension to the use of these sites was granted since it became apparent that they could serve as satellite aerodromes and should not be obstructed if required. By 27 September 1940, the Army Council permitted the construction and operation of night decoys of civil factories.

This aerial shot was taken during the spring of 1941 and shows the completed site with the view looking north. There are no buildings on the northern site. The trees of Birchall Wood were landscaped when the aerodrome was completed in September 1943 to provide better vision of the southern portion of the field. (BAE SYSTEMS)

As for Holwell Hyde, Sound City had provided the best price for some of the decoy aircraft that graced the fields next to the canvas and wood hangar. The site had to portray the effect of a working factory and therefore personnel, vehicles and aircraft should be seen. The decoy aircraft were full-size wood and canvas replicas; delivered to the site by the Target Plane Section of RAF Hook, having been designed according to the strict Air Ministry plans. A simpler two-dimensional decoy was available but Holwell Hyde appears to have had full-size replicas of Bristol Blenheim (at a cost of £151 each), Hawker Hurricane (between £50 and £80 each and built by Green Bros Garden Furniture of Hailsham), Boulton Paul Defiant (£50) and Airspeed Oxford aircraft. Certainly the smaller models could be wheeled around the site to achieve more realism. The operating costs for the decoy site were £8,800 per annum by the time of closure in June 1942.

'QF/QL'

By June 1940 Colonel Turner's department identified further improvements to the night operations of the proposed decoy sites. A night decoy was dubbed a 'Q' site with a suffix added to define a further role e.g. 'F' = fire and 'L' = lights. Turner decided it was necessary to protect certain RAF stations by using diversionary fires in an attempt to lure enemy bombers away and twenty-four such facilities were completed by November 1940, Holwell Hyde being one (QF225). The 'QF' portion of the code related to Holwell Hyde being a fire site designed for night deception activities. The role of a QF site was to protect RAF stations and expanded later to protect small civil, naval and military targets. The fire decoys consisted of drip or sputtering oil and coal fires designed to simulate flashes of fire from exploding bombs and burning buildings (often coded 'Boilers' and 'Fire Baskets'). The facility was manned and supervised by two civilian operators based on the station concerned and maintenance carried out by works personnel under supervision of the works area superintendent. Due to the importance of aircraft production, QF sites were installed close to four decoy/dummy factory sites with Holwell Hyde chosen to deter night attacks on de Havilland at Hatfield.

Real aircraft in the form of Tiger Moths from 1 EFTS at Hatfield had landed at Holwell Hyde, sometimes in error it was stated at the time because of the realistic nature of the 'factory', and the field was nicknamed 'Hogsnorton' by pilots after the fictitious village created by the comedian Gillie Potter, although reference to the name can be found nearby at Old Knebworth.

A Bristol Blenheim and two Boulton Paul Defiant decoy aircraft are placed near to the northern edge of the decoy factory, looking to the east. (BAE SYSTEMS)

Dated 16 October 1941 the photograph depicts the site structurally complete although a little untidy and shows a decoy Airspeed Oxford trainer parked facing the largest of the decoy 'hangars'. This view looks towards the west. (BAE SYSTEMS)

Here the nose of a de Havilland Moth, one of many withdrawn from use and used as decoys by Sound City Studios, is positioned next to the south-east corner of the decoy factory. Dated 23 October 1941, this is one of a series of pictures taken of the facility showing it nearing completion with camouflage painting about to take place. (BAE SYSTEMS)

With the 'QF' explained above, Holwell Hyde had the added code 'QL'. A 'QL' site was electrically lit to simulate poor blackout or the 'permitted' lighting of towns and cities up to 30 acres (12 hectares) in size. This deception involved quite sophisticated lighting techniques to confuse enemy bombers into attacking a decoy factory or railway yard, the lighting being laid out in strict patterns. Usual equipment to run the site consisted of an engine generator supplying a primary and residual electrical circuit for lighting, controlled by dimmers and adjusted to suit weather and night conditions. In operation the primary circuits switched off with the approach of an unidentified aircraft leaving a few marker lights to 'attract' bombers.

By a brutal quirk of fate the decoy facility was not operating successfully during the daytime attack by the Luftwaffe at Hatfield on 3 October 1940. The tragic bombing of the '94' Shop at de Havilland's Hatfield factory killed twenty-one people and injured seventy more. On the day of the raid, the Luftwaffe Ju 88 responsible for the bombing was hit by anti-aircraft fire and crashed at East End Green Farm about 1 mile east of Holwell Hyde.

By August 1941 the schedule of sites lists Holwell Hyde as a miscellaneous dummy building site 'M3', located at the same Map Ref.715323 (OS 1" to 1 mile No.96). The site was manned and operated by the de Havilland Aircraft Co. under the management responsibility of Mr Maslin, still acting as decoy for Hatfield under Area K8 (Uxbridge) control. The regional contractor was given as Sound City (Films) Ltd of Chertsey.

The schedule of 18 June 1942 indicated the manufacturing site as being dismantled and its status changed to civilian decoy site C99a (still ostensibly a decoy for Hatfield) with C99a

An excellent view looking north from the entrance to the site, dated 23 October 1941. Several cars, all MoT failures, adorn the site while smoke issues from the chimneys. Some canvas work is being carried out on frames to the left and right of the chimneys. In the far distance facing north-west is a decoy Hawker Hurricane. (BAE SYSTEMS)

A view now looking east toward Hertford, showing dispersed cars and the variety in shading of the canvas structures. (BAE SYSTEMS)

defining Holwell Hyde as a 'QL' facility at this time. By the middle of the following month, however, C99a was withdrawn, coinciding with the role of Holwell Hyde becoming an aerodrome proper. It is probable that the decoy factory was removed completely by September 1942 as the aerodrome developed and the need for the decoy diminished.

The decoy 'QL' site (renumbered C99b) was moved to Essendon by 2 October 1942 and located at Map Ref.709285 (OS 1" to 1 mile No.96) until May 1943 at least. This position can be transferred to the local Ordnance Survey map (OS.166) as TL264090, Larkinshill Grove, half a mile south-west of Essendonbury Farm.

The final log entry for operations at the Essendon site (28 April 1943) revealed the use of 4 gallons of petrol per week via a 3½hp JAP engine used to operate the lighting.

There is a cruel irony that the position of this site was only 100 yards east of the explosive arrival of a German V-2 rocket on 17 January 1945, which caused local casualties.

The decoy facility on its western side, roughly in the middle of Moneyhole Lane Park. The decoy Hurricane is being attended to. The canvas and frames were tethered to the ground with guy ropes at frequent intervals but these were effectively invisible from the air. (BAE SYSTEMS)

The full-size Hurricane was constructed as a kit by Green Brothers, a garden furniture company, and cost around £60. Despite the anchoring pegs, the replica could be 'wheeled' around the site to simulate movement. Holwell Hyde was a trial facility for all manner of decoy aircraft. (BAE SYSTEMS)

3

The Early Days of the Aerodrome – Holwell Hyde

OVER-SPILL FROM HATFIELD

On 22 October 1940 a Tiger Moth of 1 EFTS, R4920, collided with high-tension cables and crashed at Brickenden Bury. Two days later another, N9327, flown by L.A.C. Winters, hit a tree and crashed at Welwyn Garden City after flying in formation with other aircraft. These incidents are noteworthy since they were both close to the fledgling landing ground and the first on record. The Tiger Moths did not originate from the aerodrome but in all reality 1 EFTS probably did use Holwell Hyde by this time in its intended role as a reserve landing ground to familiarise students in landings away and had probably done so since late summer 1940. It should be noted that the Training School also used a reserve landing ground at Sandridge, to the south-west of Hatfield (Hill End Farm). The exact location was Grid Ref. TL160105 or Lat/Long N5147-W0019.

On 22 December 1940 Army HQ for the Hertford area issued instructions to Hatfield on the importance of keeping runways clean of snow on operational and dummy aerodromes. By 4 January 1941 the Operational Record Book states that a snow-clearing plan for the reserve landing ground at Holwell Hyde had been issued.

At Hatfield, peak activity for 1 EFTS was reached during 1941 when the school had forty-two instructors, five Flights and ninety aircraft (all Tiger Moths) and with this level of commitment the facilities became fully stretched. As a consequence 'B' Flight transferred to Holwell Hyde on 16 June 1941 with a complement of forty-three personnel. Under the command of Flt Lt H.J. 'Jack' Greenland (later a Mosquito production test pilot), 'B' Flight had eight Tiger Moths and, after the construction of suitable hangars, occupied the north side of the aerodrome near Bericot Green, away from the decoy facility.

The Air Ministry plan for Holwell Hyde, dated 1942, revealed four runways (all grass) positioned approximately North-South (1,000 yards or 1,800 yards after re-stripping land beyond), NE-SW (1,033 yards or 1900 yards after re-stripping), E-W (1,166 yards or 1400 yards after re-stripping) and NW-SE (1,033 yards). This layout shows the decoy facility as an administration and technical area, though by the summer of 1941 most personnel connected with 1 EFTS were billeted and trained on the north site. Two, 69' wide, steel, Miskin-designed 'Extra-Over' blister hangars were built with at least five 45' wide, wood-framed Miskin blisters. These were placed close to the runways in use at the time. The attendant huts and fuelling facilities and access route from the B1000 Welwyn–Hertford road were ready by mid-1941.

By June 1941 there is levelling of the fields and buildings appear on the northern perimeter with at least one transportable Miskin blister hangar right of centre. 'B' Flight of 1 EFTS transferred to Holwell Hyde on 16 June 1941 and the flight hut (building No.15), clothing store (No.17) and one barrack hut (No.25) are visible. (BAE SYSTEMS)

Fully equipped with a blind flying hood, this spectacular photograph of 1 EFTS Tiger Moth, N6919 (82163) taken in May 1941 is very interesting since the pilot is Prince Bernhard of the Netherlands. The prince was an avid and capable pilot who visited Holwell Hyde and Panshanger on several occasions since the EFTS trained Dutch Army and Air Force students following the invasion of their homeland by the Germans. This Tiger Moth survived many minor scrapes with the EFTS until it required a repair in works from 7 September 1943 after which it moved elsewhere. (BAE SYSTEMS)

Prince Bernhard talks to his instructor at Hatfield alongside de Havilland Tiger Moth, BB740, '46' of 1 EFTS. Individual two-digit aircraft codes were carried by 1 EFTS during the war for recognition purposes. BB740 was built at Hatfield and registered as G–AFGY on 9 May 1938 with the de Havilland School of Flying, the precursor to the Elementary and Reserve Flying Training School. Along with many others, it was impressed into military service in October 1940 and joined 1 EFTS at Hatfield. On 16 July 1941 Sgt Catley stalled on landing at Hatfield and crashed. BB740 was repaired and moved to 29 EFTS at Clyffe Pypard on 6 September 1941. (BAE SYSTEMS)

Above: The Hawker Hind was designed to be an interim replacement for the earlier Hart day bomber. 124 Hind bombers were converted by General Aircraft at Hanworth as dual control trainers from November 1937 and L7213, seen here, had been delivered to 1 EFTS at Hatfield on 1 January 1941 for the exclusive use of Prince Bernhard through January. It remained with the Unit until 4 June 1941 when it moved into storage with 8 MU. (BAE SYSTEMS)

Opposite: The earliest plan of the aerodrome is dated 1942 showing the decoy factory site to the south and four runways, the longest of 1,166 yards. By 1942 'B' Flight of 1 EFTS was situated on the north site and the dichotomy of an active training airfield aligned with a facility aiming to have bombs dropped on it could not have been more bizarre. (Author)

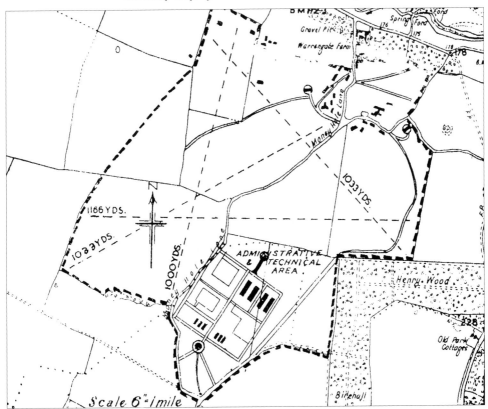

The access road entered through Warrengate Farm and up a rise, passing the guard hut and the first Link trainer building (ready by September 1942). 4,000 gallons of aviation fuel were stored in a tank, partly underground, to the right of this lane as one came onto the aerodrome.

ACCIDENTS

Sadly, the same day 'B' Flight transferred to Holwell Hyde (16 June 1941) a Tiger Moth T5834, flown by LAC Sajet (Dutch Army), crashed on the boundary of Hatfield Aerodrome and he died of his injuries next day. Three days later LAC Deroo, another Dutch Army pilot, was killed flying Tiger Moth BB736, after colliding in mid-air with a Blenheim, V6360, over Aston Clinton, Bucks. On 1 July 1941 LAC Lammas was landing at Holwell Hyde in Tiger Moth T6108 and bounced heavily causing the undercarriage to collapse, resulting in major damage.

On 27 June Flt Lt Greenland was appointed assistant CFI of 1 EFTS and F/O Stanley replaced him at Holwell Hyde being promoted to Flt Lt. Sqdn Ldr Noble, 50 Group Defence Officer (controlling 1 EFTS), visited the station on 21 July.

The toll of the intense flying training continued on 2 September with a tragic mid-air collision near Hatfield between two Tiger Moths, N6662 and N9500, flown by LAC Moore (solo) and Sgt Hainsworth/LAC Brown. The crews were killed.

On 15 October, AVM Hon. Air Commanding the Auxiliary Air Force, HRH Duke of Kent, toured the facilities at Hatfield and Holwell Hyde. Eleven days later the CO, Wg Cdr C.A. Pike AFC, and several school personnel took part in a radio programme with the BBC called *Aircrews of Tomorrow*, a recording of which was made available by December 1941. The commentators were Michael Standing, Stewart MacPherson and Wynford Vaughan Thomas.

Top: Tiger Moth T7414 was built in September 1940 by Morris Motors at Cowley and stored until issued to 1 EFTS at Hatfield on 16 August 1941, coded '43'. On 12 September 1941 Flt Lt Payne was practicing forced landing procedures at Sandridge RLG and hit a tree trunk causing the aircraft to overturn, fortunately without injury to the pilot. T7414 was repaired by February 1942 and moved to 11 EFTS Perth. (BAE SYSTEMS)

Middle: Another Tiger Moth built at Cowley by Morris Motors, T6287, coded '40' was received by 1 EFTS on 11 June 1941 and used until moved to 28 EFTS at Wolverhampton on 1 November that year. (BAE SYSTEMS)

Bottom: This view shows the early days of 'B' Flight dispersal at Holwell Hyde, September 1941. 'B' Flight's Laing hut is on the left, just behind is the camouflaged clothing store (Whitlock design) and further back the first of the barrack huts for six personnel (Laing-type). Later a ten-man hut would join it. These huts lasted until the 1990s when age and vandalism required them to be removed. (BAE SYSTEMS)

Taken in September 1941, a Tiger Moth, BB749, sits inside the wood-frame 45ft-span Miskin blister hangar on the northern boundary of Holwell Hyde. BB749 was built at Hatfield and registered on 6 August 1935 as G-ADKG, being impressed in October 1940. It was received by 'B' Flight 1 EFTS at Holwell Hyde on 29 June 1941 and used until moved to 9 EFTS at Ansty on 11 December the same year. Of interest is the canvas curtain/awning offering protection and additional space on the front of the hangar. C.H. Miskins was a local engineering company winning a design contract for these transportable and quickly erected hangars. The wood-frame structures survived into the 1980s but were wrecked around the closure of the airfield in 1992. (BAE SYSTEMS)

'B' Flight, 1 EFTS moved to Holwell Hyde in June 1941 following the construction of suitable hutting and limited facilities on the northern site. In addition to the hangar shown here, two more Miskin blister hangars were constructed on the north site, one for motor transport (MT) and the other for aircraft protection and maintenance, though the Miskin standard blister has a Tiger Moth inside it is hemmed in by vehicles. Taken on 23 October 1941, this shot shows Tiger Moths T6289 '88' and R4923 '92' picketed out near to the newly completed buildings.

The term Hogsnorton captions this photograph and comes from the mythical village created by the comedian Gillie Potter and broadcast on BBC radio during the 1930s and 1940s. In reality the official name for the aerodrome was Holwell Hyde though the pseudonym became apt for the decoy factory. (BAE SYSTEMS)

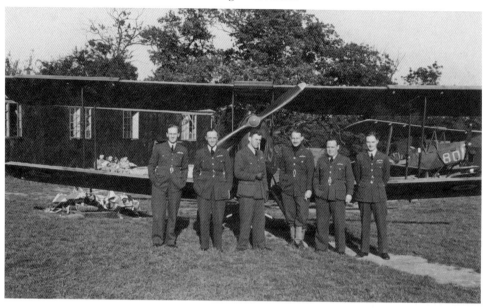

On 23 October 1941, Instructors of 'B' Flight, 1 EFTS stand in front of a Tiger Moth at Holwell Hyde. Second from right is Don MacBeath, later to join the London Aeroplane Club as an instructor. Pupils lounge against the wall of the Flight Hut awaiting their lessons. (BAE SYSTEMS)

Another view on 23 October 1941 shows Tiger Moths waiting crews. A fuel bowser is seen between two aircraft. Initially, fuel was delivered to a 4,000-gallon tank just to the right of the access road south of the guard hut but later two 12,000-gallon underground tanks were installed, located to the east of the pictured area and now covered in undergrowth. The fuel and oil facility nearby served aircraft and motor vehicles and the attendant pumps and pipework still exist.

Access to the north site was via the B1000 road from Digswell to Hertford, through Warrengate Farm and up the hill to the aerodrome. A guard room and Link Trainer building constructed at the top of the road still exist on what is now private land. Behind the flight hut would later stand the RAF Mess and barrack huts. (BAE SYSTEMS)

Again taken on 23 October 1941 showing the fairly Spartan facilities afforded to 'B' Flight. Crews were brought to the aerodrome by ground transport in the early days, there being little accommodation until the Mess was completed. The Miskin blister hangar was constructed with a wood frame and designed to be transportable and the one seen here was not the permanent denuded frame still seen today. Tiger Moth '87' pokes its nose out of the hangar. (BAE SYSTEMS)

On 15 October 1941 George, Duke of Kent, visited Hatfield to view Mosquito production and Holwell Hyde. Here he talks with a wing commander of Training Command and Cadet Kirk at Holwell Hyde, in his capacity as head of RAF Training Command, a post he served until his untimely death. In August 1942, the Duke, then age thirty-nine, was undertaking a tour of stations in his role as Air Commodore of the department of Inspector General of the RAF. On 25 August the Duke was scheduled to fly from Invergordon to Reykjavik, Iceland, in Short Sunderland, W4026 'DQ-M' of 228 Squadron Coastal Command. He was accompanied by a few staff as well as RAF crew. Heavily laden with fuel in inclement weather the aircraft crossed the Caithness coast south of the Berriedale Water and crashed into an outcrop on the northern extremity of the ridge known locally as The Eagles Rock. All but the tail gunner were killed. (BAE SYSTEMS)

On 19 April 1942 the prototype de Havilland Mosquito night fighter, W4052 force-landed at Holwell Hyde opposite the decoy facility, roughly where the wasteland is between Bericot Way and Shackleton Way. A team from Hatfield arrived to repair the Mosquito, which was soon repaired and flew out on 5 May. (BAE SYSTEMS)

MOSQUITO ACCIDENT

On 19 April 1942, during a test flight near Hatfield with the prototype DH.98 Mosquito night fighter W4052, Geoffrey de Havilland Jnr and observer Brian Cross noted the port engine running rough. After feathering the propeller they attempted to land at Hatfield but a Percival Proctor, taking off, caused them to overshoot and try again. Unfortunately the starboard engine began to overheat and they were forced to make a safe belly-landing at Holwell Hyde. The crew was unhurt and the Mosquito repaired on site from 27 April until 5 May when it flew to Hatfield.

PANSHANGER POST-NATAL HOSPITAL

As a slight aside, in June 1942 the Ministry of Housing and Local Government considered the use of Panshanger House, the former seat of the Desborough family, as a post-natal hospital staffed by the Mothercraft Training Society. The fifty beds would give preference to evacuee mothers and babies and for non-evacuees at 8s 1d a day (40p). Invitations were sent to many London hospitals and authorities with general acceptance, though the scheme appears to have been shelved quite soon afterwards.

THE MOVE TO HOLWELL HYDE

By this time (spring 1942) the requirement for the decoy facility had passed and it was clear that the heavy demands on Hatfield for Mosquito production would squeeze the training still further, therefore building had commenced in earnest at Holwell Hyde to transfer the remainder of the school later in the year. By 23 June 1942 temporary sick quarters had been built at Holwell Hyde but the main facility remained at Hatfield for the time being. Construction of the administration, training and medical facilities began on the south-east portion of the land previously unused for the aerodrome (18 acres) but would not be ready until September 1943. The western boundary of this field was a low hedge, parts of which were retained and can be seen in early photographs.

On 11 July 1942, 2nd Lt Saddleton escaped relatively unscathed from Tiger Moth BB724, which crashed at Holwell Hyde; two days later he severely damaged N6873 in similar circumstances. It was recommended that the student see an ophthalmic consultant. July also brought a mass parade of ATC cadets to Holwell Hyde; on 19 July eleven of them succumbed to the summer heat and fainted.

With the autumn approaching, 1 EFTS relocated their HQ to Tewin on 7 September, still awaiting the opening of the main station headquarters. The various Flights and Tiger Moth aircraft followed them to Holwell Hyde after the dismantling of the decoy factory. The Link Trainer Flight and ground instructional staff remained at Hatfield until the middle of 1943 when the south site had been completed.

On 14 September F/O Bednells, flying Tiger Moth T6297, collided on landing at Holwell Hyde with BB737, which was unmanned, fortunately with little damage to his aircraft. On 13 October 2nd Lt Ballyn, flying T7413, crash-landed at Holwell Hyde after stalling from 50ft. Another incident took place on 29 October 1942 when Lt Tanner and Lt Hadley landed at Holwell Hyde in Tiger Moth T7417 and collided with a parked Tiger Moth, R5082, causing major damage to both aircraft. On 1 November 100 ATC cadets attended lectures at Hatfield aerodrome, marking the beginning of a regular training course (first Sunday of the month).

On 10 December 1942 P/O J.N. Somers (120092) was attached to Holwell Hyde from 6 EFTS for night-flying instructor duties and remained until 30 December. Nat Somers would become linked closely with the aerodrome over the future years.

HOLWELL HYDE

Air Ministry files for November 1942 reveal a snapshot of the facilities at Holwell Hyde:

Grid Reference:	1in Map L715323, Sheet 96
Position:	51°47'45"N 00°09'30"W
Locality:	3½ miles North of Hatfield
Height ASL:	250ft
Flying Training Command, RLG for EFTS, Parent at Hatfield	
Other Functions:	Nil

'Suitable for light types otherwise subsidences are (sic) liable to occur without warning. Surface condition after rain is very good'

Runways:	Nil
Perimeter Track:	Nil
Type of surface:	Grass
Prevailing Wind:	SW
Obstructions:	Position of wind indicators, 1 x NW, 1 x S
	Smoke during flying hours
Fog Prevalence:	November – February 40%
	February – November 5%
Facilities:	Petrol = 4000 gallons aviation
Refuelling = Bowser & Brockhouse	

Oil = Nil, Bomb = Nil, Small Arms Ammunition = Nil, Tractors = 1, Jacks = Nil, Cranes/Hoist = Nil, Snow Plough, Rollers = 1 Bunce, 1 Johnson

Hangars:	2 Extra Over Blisters, 5 Blisters
Night Landing Facilities:	Nil
Radio:	Nil
Blind Approach:	Nil
QDM:	Nil
Met:	Nil
Scale:	Reserve Landing Ground
Availability:	For emergency use only
Dispersal; Limited	
Essential Buildings = NA	
Transport:	Bus Hertford to Tewin hourly

4

1943

After dark on 12 March 1943 a Wellington 1C of 14 OTU, Z1154, crashed at Holwell Hyde after the pilot, Sgt Powell, had reported engine trouble. The aircraft overshot the flare path, hit barbed wire entanglements and came to rest in trees on the aerodrome boundary, fortunately without injury to the crew of six.

On 7 April a severe gale damaged hangars and aircraft on the northern site, while on 15 April two Tiger Moths collided during taxiing. Fortunately, 23 April saw the start-up of the Aircraft Repair section at Holwell Hyde. Later the same month and during early May, two defence exercises were undertaken, 'Tewin' (spelt 'Tewen' in the ORB) on 29 April and 'Holwell' on 18 May. Designed to simulate an invasion by enemy parachutists, the 'attacking' force of 'desperate German paratroops' was fulfilled by the Worcestershire Regiment equipped with a Carrier and Mortar section and defences manned by 1 EFTS and Home Guard personnel, the expected attacks coming from the southern perimeter. A gas attack exercise was carried out on 27 May with a mustard gas mine being set off on the aerodrome and it is assumed that all went well.

On 14 May 1943 Cpl Hatfield landed heavily at Holwell Hyde causing Tiger Moth T7735 to tip onto its nose, resulting in major damage.

THE SITE IS COMPLETED

The new administration block on the south side was officially opened on 11 June 1943 along with the new training buildings, canteen and attendant facilities and most staff relocated from Hatfield. Four days later two Tiger Moths, piloted solo by AOP students, collided prior to landing, one crash-landing in an adjoining field, the other relatively safely on the runway. On the evening of 23 June the air-raid sirens were sounded and a lone Focke Wulf 190, chased by a Mosquito night fighter, dropped two bombs, which fell 100 yards outside the southern boundary of the aerodrome, with little damage being caused. By 21 July Wg Cdr Clement Pike AFC had returned from RAF Mount Batten to resume command of 1 EFTS. Three days later another Tiger Moth, EM813, crashed injuring F/O Gabb and Lt Gray after they force-landed at Bramfield, 1½ miles to the north east.

During the summer, students and staff could enjoy swimming at Hatfield or Tewin Water House (by kind permission of Lady Biet).

The Percival Proctor was a three to four-seat communication, liaison and radio trainer used by the RAF during the war. 1 EFTS had a few (four + one reserve) for Link Trainer duties by training the instructors in flying and using instruments, the so-called 'L' Flight. The Link Trainer was a ground-based simulator that allowed a student to become aware of controls and instruments in the security of a controlled environment. Holwell Hyde had a Link Trainer on the north site, the building now part of Warrengate Farm. The south site building is partly in Henry Wood and was completed when the aerodrome became known as Panshanger. The Central Link Trainer School was based at Elstree during the war and relocated late to Panshanger only after the south site was completed.

Proctor I, R7524, served with 'L' Flight, 1 EFTS during the war and was sold on 14 November 1946 to become G-AIWA. It is seen here at Sywell in 1982 repainted in wartime colours. Sadly it crashed at La Ferte Alais, France on 9 June 1984 and was not rebuilt. (Author)

A VISITING MARAUDER

The USAAF paid an unannounced visit to Holwell Hyde on 12 August when a Martin B-26 Marauder made a precautionary landing after problems occurred during an operational flight. Two Tiger Moths were lost during August; on 12 August Flt Lt Piddock landed heavily at Holwell Hyde in DE297, causing substantial damage, while on 17 August Lt Bowden spun into the ground in DE711 near Litchborough, Northants, after a flight from Hatfield. This incident was subject to a Court of Inquiry at Holwell later.

AIR TRAINING CORPS

127 Elementary Gliding School was formed at Holwell Hyde on 16 June 1943 to provide air cadets with air experience flying, although their hardware (in the form of a Slingsby Cadet glider) did not arrive for another two months.

Throughout the summer Air Training Corps squadrons from the local Hertfordshire units visited the field for training, flying experience and Camp, tented accommodation usually. 1166 Squadron (Welwyn Garden City) and 795 Squadron (Harpenden) archives recall air experience flights for cadets in Airspeed Oxford and de Havilland Dominie aircraft. Cadets could watch a Dakota towing a Horsa glider and an air display by a Hawker Typhoon. Link trainer operations could be observed and basic aircraft engineering practice was taught.

RAF STATION PANSHANGER

The official name change from Holwell Hyde to RAF Station Panshanger occurred on 13 September 1943, following completion of the south site. In the official diary for the month, 1 EFTS was equipped with Tiger Moth, Austers and Proctors for the purposes of training Army personnel to pilot status. Two Link Trainer Flights were now established split to the north and south station areas. On 24 September and later on 5 November the AOC of 50 Group, Air Commodore Lockyer, visited the station.

By now, at the height of the war, 1 EFTS had 108 aircraft and forty instructors on strength.

On 1 November 1943, forty-two Turkish Air Force officers arrived for training at Hatfield and Panshanger and because of security implications it was noted that should any of the foreign officers fall sick they should be treated at Hill End Emergency Medical Station (EMS), rather than using the station facilities. Members of the Bolivian Air Mission visited Panshanger just after Christmas that year.

In poor weather at Panshanger on 3 April 1944 Turkish officers are assembled during a passing-out parade. Forty-two officers passed through 1 EFTS from 1 November 1943 until 1944. (BAE SYSTEMS)

5

1944

26 January 1944 brought another dignitary to Panshanger, Air Marshall Sir Philip Babington KCB MC AFC, AOC of Flying Training Command, who toured the aerodrome.

On 10 February 1944 another unscheduled arrival by a Wellington occurred when T2922 of 28 Operational Training Unit (OTU) at Wymeswold force-landed after the port engine was reported to have caught fire. The pilot, Sgt J.J.W. Dawson, had ordered the crew to bale out prior to landing but in the event only the mid-upper gunner, Sgt Wilkinson, was able to do so and he landed in a tree nearby. The remainder of the crew stayed with the aircraft, now too low for them to parachute safely and fortunately all walked free from the aircraft after the safe landing. Sgt Wilkinson was waylaid for a while, suspended from branches, when a group of Turkish students approached offering (in Turkish) to help. Not being conversant in the language and no doubt thinking the worst about landing in enemy-occupied Europe he remained willingly trapped until persuaded to come down by aerodrome personnel. The Wellington was repaired on site and flown out later. On 26 March 1944 T2922 operated a mine-laying sortie over France and was attacked by a night fighter. It returned to base but was damaged beyond repair.

GERMAN BOMBS

During the night of 18 February an air-raid alert sounded and two canisters of 1kg incendiaries (some 1,200 bombs in all) were dropped by a German bomber in the south-west corner of the aerodrome (Attimore Hall), with 700 falling on the field itself. Haystacks in the adjoining fields were set alight but little other damage was done and the aerodrome returned to operational status later the following day.

On the social side the RAF Mess was entertained on 7 March by the dance band the 'Skyrockets', formed from members of No.1 Balloon Centre, and on 17 March Gp Capt. E.A.C. Britton DFC, the new AOC of 50 Group, visited the aerodrome.

On 14 March 1944 Lt Toros, a Turkish Air Force student, got lost during a cross-country in Tiger Moth, T6769 and put down in a field 1 mile west of the brickworks at Elstow, Bedfordshire. He ran out of runway on take off and parked in a hedge, damaging the aircraft severely.

A medical alert occurred on 24 March when a smallpox outbreak in Hertfordshire required all personnel to be vaccinated. The de Havilland Aircraft Co.'s founders, Sir Geoffrey de Havilland and Frank Hearle, visited Panshanger at the end of the month. In early April,

Major maintenance being carried out on Tiger Moth, N9432, at Panshanger on 24 February 1944. The south site was fully functional around September 1943 and the servicing carried out under relatively good conditions with modern facilities. The de Havilland Technical School used these facilities for much of its 'hands-on' apprentice training in airframes, engines and aircraft systems. (BAE SYSTEMS)

After the rebuild in February 1944, Tiger Moth N9432, coded '16', is being hand swung, parked between the two Miskin blister hangars on the south site. N9432 was built at Hatfield and joined 1 EFTS there on 23 November 1940. On 24 July 1945 it was damaged beyond repair after turning over on landing at Panshanger. (BAE SYSTEMS)

Inspection of the business end of a Tiger Moth, its 130hp Gipsy Major engine. The air-cooled four-cylinder in-line ran inverted, i.e. the crankshaft was at the top and the pistons aimed downwards. A clever design of oil galleries and oil feed ensured that all the right parts got the right amounts of lubricant, preferably at the right time. The reason for running inverted should be obvious from the position of the propeller, which is well clear of the ground, with visibility for the crew much better over the top of the engine. The Gipsy Major was arguably the most successful light aeroplane engine of its time, very reliable, robust and affordable. In a strange quirk of its lineage, its family tree goes back to the French Renault V-8 of the First World War; the Gipsy Major has many metric threaded nuts and studs but uses Whitworth heads, made suitable for most UK toolkits at the time. (BAE SYSTEMS)

An aerial view of the south site on 10 September 1944 showing the year-old site, including the aircraft-shaped headquarters in the foreground. (BAE SYSTEMS)

following completion of their training course, the Turkish officers paraded at Panshanger in the presence of AVM Paxton DFC, Gp Capt. Britton and Capt. Dirvana of the Turkish Air Attache. The Turks later entertained the instructors at the Stone House Hotel, Hatfield. The new Station Sick Quarters was opened the same day, 3 April 1944, situated to the east of the administration building on the south side.

On 12 May F/O Greenwood and P/O Walker undershot a landing at Panshanger flying NL823 and collided with a windsock, wrecking the Tiger Moth.

THE AIR TRAINING CORPS GLIDERS

On 16 June, the same day a V1 fell on Sandridge, 127 Elementary Gliding School (EGS) was established at Panshanger to commence glider training of ATC cadets and located themselves in the far south-west corner of the aerodrome, utilising a blister hangar. The school equipped with Grunau Baby and Slingsby Cadet I and II gliders and continued to operate until 30 May 1948. Later the site was used by 122 EGS (under 64 Group, Reserve Command) from October 1951 until 1955, flying the Slingsby TX3 glider. This group was based at Halton and eventually renamed 613 Venture Gliding School. The land used by the school, on the southern tip of the aerodrome, is now part of the Moneyhole Lane Park and all evidence of its former existence has been removed.

Royal visitors toured Panshanger on 6 July 1944; HM King Peter of Yugoslavia and HRH Prince Bernhard of the Netherlands arrived by air in the Prince's Beech 17 and returned on 26 September. ATC summer camps began in July and ACM Sir Charles Burnett visited the EGS and the camp to meet cadets who were provided with flying opportunities throughout August in visiting Oxford and Dominie aircraft .

6

1945 and the Final Year of War

The severe winter of 1944–45 curtailed much flying but the New Year was highlighted with the award of a unit badge by HRH King George VI on 31 January, which consisted of a Tiger Moth emerging from a chrysalis carrying the motto *ab initio*.

On 21 February 1945 Army 2nd glider pilots commenced flying training. The first flying incident of 1945 occurred on 13 April when Cpl Simmonds stalled on landing at Panshanger and crashed, flying Tiger Moth T6298. Three days later Cpl Mills crash-landed in T6435 after the rudder jammed.

The European war drew to a close and Wg Cdr Pike took the salute at the VE Day parade in May 1945. 13 June 1945 saw Flt Lt J.N. Somers AFC return to 1 EFTS to take up attachment as a flying instructor. On 23 July Cpl Malcolm, flying DE679, crash-landed and the following day three Tiger Moths were severely damaged in separate incidents. N9330, flown by Cpl Jones, landed heavily and broke the undercarriage and similarly disfigured was N9432, flown by Cpl Burman, and N5444. The final incident of the wartime training activities occurred on 31 July when F/O Costin and Cpl Saville undershot a landing at the reserve landing ground at Sandridge.

PEACETIME

With the end of the war, 1 EFTS took account of their successes. Some 4,800 pupils had passed through the school since 3 September 1939 and 1,000 Link Trainer pilots had completed their courses. On the anniversary of the Battle of Britain, 15 September, the CO's parade was climaxed with a flying display where Geoffrey de Havilland Jnr demonstrated the Vampire and Pat Fillingham a Mosquito. The end of 1945 saw the first performance at Panshanger of the play *With knobs on*, produced by Flt Lt Page with 1 EFTS personnel support.

With the inevitable run down of training requirements after the war, 1 EFTS reduced its flying throughout 1946 and allied to this fewer social activities were recorded. In April 1946 127 EGS held school camps for sixteen ATC cadets and three officers. The Gliding School became part of 61 Group RAF on 20 May 1946.

Right: The squadron badge allotted to 1 EFTS.
(1166 (WGC) Squadron Air Training Corps)

Below: 1166 (Welwyn Garden City) Squadron
Air Training Corps is based in Lemsford Lane
WGC and visits to the aerodrome during and
after the war were plentiful. HQ Herts Air
Cadets was based at Panshanger enabling cadet
flying training and ground school of the like that
probably cannot be repeated. Here a squadron
corporal and flight sergeant are being instructed
in the business end of the Tiger Moth, its Gipsy
Major engine, by a Reserve Flying School
instructor. The photograph was taken in 1947.
(1166 (WGC) Squadron Air Training Corps)

Left: Ken Green adjusts his parachute prior to going aboard a Tiger Moth in 1947. The Tiger Moth in the background is DE637 of 1 RFS, coded RCM-D. It remained at Panshanger until transferred to 25 RFS Wolverhampton on 29 June 1950, Ken remained considerably longer. (1166 (WGC) Squadron Air Training Corps)

Below: ATC cadet Ken Green poses in the cockpit of 1 RFS Tiger Moth, T7728. This photograph comes from a series taken at Panshanger in 1947, shortly after the RFS was formed, and the Tiger Moth still carries the 1 EFTS code FHB-C. It later carried the proper RFS code RCM-W. The aircraft moved to storage at 10 MU Hullavington on 31 October 1950. Ken Green ran the well-known Motor Cycle shop in Haldens and owned and flew many light aircraft at Panshanger, including Piper Vagabond, G-AWOH, Stampe G-AXCZ and Emeraude, G-ASLX. (1166 (WGC) Squadron Air Training Corps)

127 Gliding School was based at Panshanger from August 1943 until May 1948 and used several cadet gliders for instruction of ATC cadets. In 1947 cadets of 1166 (WGC) Squadron Air Training Corps were being given tuition prior to a bungee launch in Kirkby (Slingsby) Cadet 1, VM591. VM591 was new in March 1947 and remained with the school until damaged on 12 December 1948. (1166 (WGC) Squadron Air Training Corps)

The Kirkby (Slingsby) Cadet TX.1 was the first training glider used, the Elementary Gliding Schools assisting many Air Training Corps cadets to get their gliding brevets. From 1943 until 1948 127 EGS occupied a blister hangar in the extreme southern corner of what is now Moneyhole Lane Park almost adjacent to the entrance road from Blackfan Road to the decoy facility. HQ Herts Wing Air Cadets was based at Panshanger and the aerodrome would provide gliding and powered flying for many local squadrons and in summer time the week-long camp would enable cadets to fly for nothing in a variety of visiting aircraft. The Gliding School operated a few Kirkby Cadets, which were bungee-launched from ground catapults, and in the summer of 1947 PD632 awaits the slack to be taken up. (1166 (WGC) Squadron Air Training Corps)

7

1946 – Civilian Flying Begins

The wartime restrictions on civilian flying were eased at the start of 1946 and by March a permit to fly was issued to selected clubs. The London Aeroplane Club re-opened for business on 12 April 1946, transferring from the pre-war Hatfield site and occupying premises on the north side of the aerodrome, where 'B' Flight 1 EFTS had started operations. Being housed on an active RAF site, the club had access to a bar and restaurant. The RAF Flying Club, likewise, commenced flying that month. The club secretary, Flt Lt Thomas, was also an instructor with the reserve school and Officer Commanding 220 (Hatfield and St Albans) ATC Squadron.

On the social side, an entertaining game of cricket on 28 May revealed the station playing Central Link Trainer School (CLTS), Elstree, and scoring 151 runs. Elstree went to bat and were bowled out for nine, with F/O Rayner-Sharpe taking six wickets for one run!

During August AVM Sir Harry Broadhurst visited the station.

1946 was not without tragedy and on 17 October Flt Lt L.N. Empson and Lt G.A. Greenwood (RCN), flying Tiger Moth, T7615, were killed in a mid-air collision with an Airspeed Oxford, RR336 of 12 MU, 1 mile west of Sandridge.

1947

Over the period from 6–13 March 1947, the aerodrome suffered a conflagration of swallow holes (called 'money holes', hence the local name), which appeared without warning after a heavy snowfall had melted. At least forty holes were recorded, the largest being 6ft across and 2ft deep. Since the site had been built on moraine deposit from the glacial outwash of the Ice Age Mimram River (its southern bank), it was and still is prone to this form of activity. In the early days of the construction of housing at Panshanger where swallow holes were encountered many delays were caused to the building. The aerodrome was re-opened later and training continued.

THE RESERVE FLYING SCHOOL IS FORMED

Training days under the auspices of the RAF were numbered and on 5 May 1947 the school returned to Reserve Flying, becoming 1 RFS under direct management from the de Havilland Aeronautical Technical School. Volunteer Reserve pilots and crews under the authority of 65 Group Royal Air Force operated the Tiger Moth, and later the Chipmunk and the Avro Anson.

Taken on 11 July 1947, this shot shows the north site and the extent of hutting. The area was largely used by the London Aeroplane Club to the left side and Avro Anson dispersal in the large steel-frame Miskin hangar. (BAE SYSTEMS)

In 1947 Tiger Moth R4973, RCM-S of 1 RFS, was the first to emerge from the Aircraft Repair Shop (ARS) (Building 46), in the new silver dope finish with yellow 'trainer' band on the rear fuselage. This replaced the all-over yellow used in the immediate post-war years. R4973 went into storage at 10 MU Hullavington, August 1950. (A.R. 'Pop' Bilkey)

The ARS in December 1948 with a rash of Tiger Moth parts. Wings of R5103 and EM920 are evident. DH Technical School students Alan Nash and Mike Rogers face the camera. (A.R. 'Pop' Bilkey)

Training continued, with ATC cadets being given their first taste of air experience flying and apprentices, the fundamental skills of aeronautical engineering, in the school facilities on the southern portion of the aerodrome. As noted above, the old 'B' Flight hangars at Bericot Green became the base for the London Aeroplane Club with the large 'L' Flight Miskin blister to the north-east boundary being occupied by the 1 RFS Anson T.21 aircraft.

An RAF photo-reconnaissance shot of Panshanger, taken in August 1947, reveals use of the same runways as during the war with a similar number of hangars.

Wg Cdr Clement (Clem) A.P. Pike AFC, a First World War DH.4 pilot who became an instructor in 1927 and commanded the EFTS from 1935, continued to do so with the RFS. During the post-war period the RFS instructors were Sqdn Ldr E.B. Stanhope AFC, Sqdn Ldr Don H. MacBeath, Flt Lt A.P. Lyons, Flt Lt D.A. Twyman, Flt Lt H.W. Wrighe DFC, Sqdn Ldr E.H. Buxton, and Wg Cdr W.B. Wilson. Flt Lt J.V. Paton operated as Air Traffic Controller at Panshanger.

Above: Looking out of the ARS hangar in 1947. LAC Hornet Moth G-AEET is undergoing an overhaul for its C of A and outside is Tiger Moth G-AHIZ. (A.R. 'Pop' Bilkey)

Left: De Havilland Technical School students, from left to right: David Bayne, Pat Hatswell and Mike Rogers are instructed by engineer R.J. 'Jacko' Jackson (extreme right). (A.R. 'Pop' Bilkey)

Opposite above: On 25 January 1948 Panshanger hosted an inspection by the C in C 65 Group Training Command. The CFI put in a sprightly display of Tiger Moth flying with this shot captured for posterity. The control tower is seen to the left. The hedgerow that formed the boundary between the aerodrome decoy site, 1942 'B' Flight aerodrome and the land acquired to build the south site is seen in the centre. This was not completely removed until the 1980s. (BAE SYSTEMS)

Opposite below: The C in C inspection in January 1948 showing officers and students of 1 RFS and their Tiger Moth aircraft. During the war 1 EFTS had used individual aircraft codes consisting of two numbers. Later in the war this altered to four letters with 1 EFTS using FHAA to FHAZ, FHBA to FHBZ and FHCA to FHCZ. Post-war, 1 RFS used RCMA to RCMZ on Tiger Moth and Chipmunk aircraft (at first). Initially Ansons used RCM with an individual aircraft number. (BAE SYSTEMS)

On 19 June 1948, de Havilland photographer Jim Mead was able to take several air to air shots of 1 RFS Tiger Moths during a sortie from the aerodrome. Flown by Mr Sinclair, R4973, coded RCM-S, served with 1 EFTS during 1943, moving to Halton briefly before returning to Panshanger and transferring to 1 RFS in 1947. It was pensioned off in 1950 and stored at 10 MU Hullavington. (Jim Mead)

A Tiger Moth formation showing N9510 (RCM-F) which was delivered to 1 RFS on 25 January 1948 and served until transferred to 11 RFS at Perth on 23 June 1950 when Panshanger received its Chipmunk trainers. EM920 (RCM-J) had been delivered to 1 EFTS in March 1944 and served with 1 RFS until downgraded for instructional use, becoming 6791M on 28 September 1950. (Jim Mead)

8

1948 and Beyond

On 9 May 1948 a large formation of 601 and 604 Squadron aircraft from the Auxiliary Air Force over-flew Panshanger en route to Hendon. During that month pilot E.J. Price was taxiing Tiger Moth DE412 and collided with an aircraft of the London Aeroplane Club. Finally, also in May, F/O Trobe had to force land DE836 at Mossbury during a flight from Panshanger and the Tiger Moth turned over. The pilot was not hurt.

The 30 May 1948 saw the disbandment of 127 Gliding School; most of its duties was transferred to other gliding schools, mainly 122 EGS, which visited the aerodrome from Halton until the closure of the RFS in 1953.

During August 1948 Tiger Moths EM920 and DE412 collided during taxiing at Panshanger. In October Sqdn Ldr Buxton and F/O Wilson were flying T5429 near the aerodrome when the engine failed and they made a safe landing. During November F/O Roberts was flying DE836 solo and got lost returning to the aerodrome, overshot and landed at Cheddington after running out of fuel.

In June 1949 PII R.B. Martin came down safely after he force-landed T7862 at Boston, Lincolnshire. During the following month PII R.E.N. Speller force-landed in K2601 at Keevil Aerodrome, near Trowbridge, and while manoeuvring afterwards the Tiger Moth overturned. The pilot was unhurt but the Tiger had seen better days.

On 16 November 1949 Anson VV252 was taxiing at Panshanger under the command of PII D. Stoneham when the ground subsided under the starboard undercarriage, causing damage. On 27 November Flt Lt Lines and F/O Pullman were carrying out a force-landing practice and hit the ground a little too heavily. R4973 took off again but the undercarriage gave up on the subsequent return to *terra firma* at Panshanger. The same day an Anson VV251 suffered an engine failure near the aerodrome and F/O R.F. Brook made a successful emergency landing, being commended for his skill.

In February 1950 F/O Foster, flying NL826 on a solo cross-country, lost his map in flight and made a successful landing at North Luffenham. Anson VV902 suffered an engine failure the same month with the crew making a safe landing at Panshanger.

CHIPMUNKS

On 15 June 1950 the school received its first de Havilland Chipmunk aircraft, which was accepted by Wg Cdr Pike. Earlier, on 8 April 1950, the Under Secretary of State for Air Mr Aidan

The RFS re-equipped with the de Havilland Canada DHC-1 Chipmunk in June 1950, replacing the venerable Tiger Moth as a primary trainer. 1 RFS used the type for three years until closure of the school in March 1953. Taken on 2 July 1950 this publicity shot for the *de Havilland Gazette* shows instructors and students on the south site with their new aircraft. (BAE SYSTEMS)

Conservative MP The Rt Hon. Aidan Crawley inspects a de Havilland Chipmunk for 1 RFS at Panshanger, 8 April 1950. WB586, coded '16', was not handed over officially until 13 July 1950. It was used until it was stored at 20 MU at Aston Down on 13 February 1953. (BAE SYSTEMS)

Taken at Panshanger on a cold 27 January 1952, the photograph is simply captioned 'Top Brass'. WB672 joined 1 RFS on 22 June 1950 and was coded '20' by the time the photograph was taken. 1 RFS used the codes RCM-A – RCM-Z, following earlier practice, but changed to two numbers later. The Chipmunk was used until stored at 22 MU Silloth on 25 February 1953. (BAE SYSTEMS)

Crawley MP flew to Panshanger in a de Havilland Devon to inspect the new type. The venerable Tiger Moths, having served the school for eighteen years, began to be supplemented during the summer of 1950 but the sound of the Gipsy Major engine continued in the Chipmunk.

ANSONS

As mentioned earlier, the school flew the Avro Anson T.21 from 1947 until its closure, this aircraft being used as a flying classroom for training navigators and engineers. The T.21 was the ultimate development of the venerable Anson and operated with reasonable safety from the aerodrome. There were two serious accidents involving the type at Panshanger, however. One such occurred on 11 November 1950 when Sqdn Ldr Rae, piloting Anson VV256, overshot a landing on the aerodrome and swung to avoid some buildings. The undercarriage was torn off and the Anson severely damaged but fortunately no injuries were reported to the crew of five.

Operation of the Reserve Flying School came under direct control of 65 Group (London Reserve) Reserve Command and participated in a number of displays and competitions with other schools during the year. On 17 June 1950 1 RFS Panshanger romped home easy winners in competition held at Redhill, with the home team, 15 RFS, 17 RFS Hornchurch and 18 RFS Fairoaks. In a series of navigation and signalling, formation flying, aerobatics and spot landing tests, 1 RFS was placed first with Redhill coming second. Anson and Tiger Moths were used.

By 1 February 1951 control of the RFS transferred to 61 Group (Eastern Reserve) after 65 Group was disbanded.

On 16 June 1951 F/O Hale and passenger R.H. Wood, flying Tiger Moth N6664, force-landed in a field near to the aerodrome and collided with a hedge, wrecking the aircraft. On 2 September 1951, with the assistance of the RFS and de Havilland Aircraft Co., Hertfordshire's Air Training Corps held their Wing Rally at Panshanger with all seventeen squadrons of the Wing participating in marching parade. The public enclosure entertained some 3,000 people who watched a flying display by 1 RFS Ansons and Chipmunks, parachuting and jet aerobatics by a Meteor and Vampire. A glider of 122 EGS was also displayed. 122 EGS were based at Halton at this time but occasionally used Panshanger in its role as HQ Air Cadets.

The Avro Anson T.21 was the final version in the highly successful series of twin-engine military and civil aircraft. Designed in 1934 as a light bomber, trainer and communication aircraft, the Anson did almost anything demanded of it. 1 RFS received seven aircraft for navigation training from 1950, all based at Panshanger for three years until the closure of the school. Ansons used the former 'L' Flight blister hangar on the north site which was later used by Agricultural Aviation and later Keegan Aviation. VV901 was delivered to 1 RFS on 1 June 1949, coded '55' and used until moved to 23 MU at Aldergrove in February 1953 for storage. It still survives and is currently under restoration at Elvington with the Yorkshire Air Museum. (MAP)

A set of aerial photographs of Panshanger was taken on Tuesday 7 March 1950 and this view, looking west, shows 1 RFS Tiger Moths parked neatly, awaiting activities. The canvas front to the blister hangar can be seen clearly in the lower portion of the frame, providing extra space and comfort for ground crew. The canvas was secured to steel rings on a track set into the concrete. These are still evident today. (BAE SYSTEMS)

The same day looking east towards Hertford shows a complete view of the military area of 1950 Panshanger. The white station HQ and administration block with the small watch tower on the north wall and signals square in front. The two large blister hangars were for aircraft storage and maintenance, the workshop for engine repairs is seen along the rear wall of one. In front of this is the medical centre, restaurant and various crew rooms (Handcraft huts). These survived until 1993 but being made of compressed asbestos were disposed of. Other buildings are described in the text. Sitting by a flight hut is an Avro Anson T.21 navigation trainer of 1 RFS. (BAE SYSTEMS)

A special event featured a Chipmunk flown by Sqdn Ldr V.R. Moon, who by radio link to the ground performed aerobatics at the personal request of members of the public.

The other accident to an Anson occurred on 24 October 1951. P/O W.H. Harris landed normally at Panshanger in VV891, but then the port undercarriage leg collapsed due to fatigue, fortunately without injuring the four crew and two passengers. The final serious flying accident at the school occurred on 5 May 1952 when P/O Stanley stalled and crashed at Panshanger in Tiger Moth EM836, which turned over.

THE RFS CLOSES

Just prior to Christmas 1952 the Air Ministry announced the closure of the Reserve Flying Schools. On 31 March 1953, thirty years after it opened (as de Havilland School of Flying), 1 RFS closed and its aircraft were dispersed.

9

Civilian Operations – The End of War and Beyond

NEWMAN AIRWAYS

Newman Airways was formed at the end of 1945, and based at Panshanger. Newman purchased ex-service Proctors with the intention of civil commercial service and by May 1946 the first converted Proctor was in use. By December 1946 a second was in service, providing ad hoc charter work. Three GAL Cygnets were purchased in 1946 from the RAF and converted for civil use and the first entered service in August 1946. Newman Aircraft was managed by Mr W. W. Lyle and Mr J. F. S. Perren and had ambitions to become an airline. Larger equipment and early success in Channel Island work meant the transfer of the company to Croydon by the summer of 1947.

THE LONDON AEROPLANE CLUB

The London Aeroplane Club was formed at Stag Lane in 1925 under the auspices of the de Havilland Aircraft Co. With 362 members (205 flying), flying instructors Francis Sparks and Sydney St Barbe, the club were in the fortunate position of receiving the highly successful DH.60 Moth from 1926 onwards. When de Havilland moved to Hatfield the club was re-established in new surroundings with a fine clubhouse and maintenance facilities, shared with the de Havilland Reserve School of Flying (later to become 1 EFTS), the Aeronautical Technical School and the RAF Flying Club. Naturally, the London Aeroplane Club used aircraft of de Havilland origin with a variety of Moths, Tiger Moths and Hornet Moths on strength up to the start of the war. Their first Moth Minor, G-AFOM, was received on 31 August 1939 but following the delivery of a few more the war then curtailed all club flying.

As mentioned earlier, the wartime restrictions on civilian flying eased during the early part of 1946 and the London Aeroplane Club re-opened for business at Panshanger on 12 April 1946, establishing itself in the northern part of the field at Bericot Green where formerly 'B' Flight 1 EFTS had been located. Initially the Hornet Moth G-AEET and Tiger Moth G-AHIZ formed the 'fleet', with another Hornet Moth, two Tiger Moths and an Auster under overhaul. Costs were high, rates of £5.10.0 per hour (£5.50) for tuition and rations of 60 gallons of petrol per aircraft per month restricted flying. The club had thirty flying members, including two student pilots, being charged 3 guineas (£3.15) entrance fee, an annual 3 guineas for membership and the flying charge. Being an RAF aerodrome, Panshanger offered a bar and restaurant to the club members as well. During May 1946 the charges were reduced from the

The Percival P.31 Proctor IV was designed as a larger version of the standard communication and radio trainer for the RAF, most being built by F. Hills & Sons at Manchester. G-AJTP served as NP281 with the 4 Radio School before being civilianised and registered on 21 April 1947 to Newman Aircraft at Panshanger. Newman Airways operated briefly from the aerodrome before moving to Croydon. 'JTP was sold to Willis Hole Aviation in August 1950. (Richard Riding)

This classic de Havilland photograph from 21 July 1947 shows Hornet Moth G-ADKW, over the London Aeroplane Club base on the northern side of the airfield. The fleet is on the grass below: Tiger Moths, G-AHXB and G-AHXC, Taylorcraft Plus D, G-AHGW and another Hornet Moth, G-ADMT. In the distance is a Moth Minor of the RAF Flying Club. (BAE SYSTEMS)

pre-war rates to £3.10.0 per hour (£3.50) for both dual and solo and the club opened every day, except Mondays and Tuesdays, from 10.00 a.m. until sunset.

The fleet was being augmented during May and now consisted of three Hornet Moths (G-ADUR, G-ADMT, G-AEET), with a fourth (G-ADKW) arriving in July and a Tiger Moth. Two Tiger Moths (G-AHXB and G-AHXC) and an Auster were delivered in July. The secretary, Wg Cdr J.A. Harris, who became aerodrome control officer at Panshanger, could be contacted on Essendon 305.

G-ADKW was registered on 9 April 1936, joining the London Aeroplane Club in August 1938. It was impressed into military service during the war as W5754 and civilianised in May 1946 to rejoin the club at Panshanger on 21 July that year. It remained flying from Panshanger until it was withdrawn from use on 14 July 1948 and was broken up for spares during 1950. (BAE SYSTEMS)

Registered in June 1936 and surviving the war, G-ADMT was used by the London Aeroplane Club at Panshanger from March 1946, one of their first post-war aircraft. It was sold to the Cardiff Aero Club in April 1952. The photograph was one of a small series identifying the handover of the club in July 1947 to the control of the de Havilland Aeronautical Technical School. From left to right is Mr E.J. Mann (DHATS), Flt Lt Dennis Cather AFM (Club CFI), Wg Cdr J.A. Harris (aerodrome control officer), Wg Cdr Clement A. Pike AFC (aerodrome manager, Hatfield) and Sqdn Ldr Robert W. Reeve DFC AFC MM (Principal of the DHATS). The new charter allowed better financial support for the club in the difficult post-war period. (BAE SYSTEMS)

THE RAF FLYING CLUB

On 13 April 1946 the RAF Flying Club reopened for business at Panshanger, having operated previously from Hatfield. The Moth Minor formed the backbone of the club's flying in the months following.

De Havilland DH.87B Hornet Moth G-ADUR was registered to the London Aeroplane Club in April 1946 at Panshanger and is seen there in the late 1940s. It was sold to L.W. Flack in March 1955 and moved away but during March 1976 Spencer Flack became the aircraft's registered owner, its base being listed as Panshanger. This was later amended to Shenley. (APN)

Another of the London Aeroplane Club Hornet Moths, G-AEET, had seen wartime military service as X9319. It was sold to the club at Panshanger on 2 April 1946 where it was photographed and used until its certificate of airworthiness lapsed on 13 August 1948. John Cooper acquired 'EET and rebuilt it at Panshanger by May 1952. (Richard Riding)

Probably one of the most well-known Moth Minors, G-AFOJ (9407) was built at Hatfield as a cabin (coupe) version and registered on 21 July 1939. De Havilland flew the aircraft under Class 'B' markings as E-0236 and during the war it became a hack and communications machine. In 1946 it was re-serialled 'E1' and in June 1949 passed to the London Aeroplane Club at Panshanger as G-AFOJ. The photograph shows the club 'winged comet' badge and a race number '50' on the fin, dating this picture to 16 September 1950 when 'FOJ was entered by the club in the *Daily Express* International Air Race, flown by Pat Fillingham. The race started at Hurn and proceeded over all the South Coast resorts to Herne Bay. Lancing College in the background identifies the location as Shoreham. 'FOJ is currently located at Salisbury Hall, having been lovingly restored there by the dedicated team. (MAP)

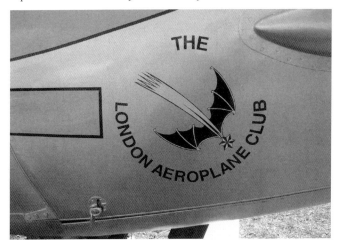

The 'winged comet' badge of the London Aeroplane Club applied to the restored G-AFOJ at Salisbury Hall, London Colney. (Author)

This Eddie Riding shot at Panshanger shows RAF Flying Club DH.94 Moth Minor G-AFNJ (94038). De Havilland Technical School student John Cooper purchased 'FNJ later and it remained based until sold in France in May 1954, becoming F-BAOG. (Richard Riding)

Pre-war de Havilland Moth Minor G-AFNJ served with the Cambridge Aero Club, having been registered in July 1939. From 1940 it was impressed as AW113, surviving until registered to the RAF Flying Club at Panshanger in June 1946, though the photograph is dated 13 April 1946, the day the RAF Flying Club was reformed after the war. Visible in the photograph are Tiger Moths R5251 (a visitor) and N6797, which transferred to 1 RFS in May 1947. (BAE SYSTEMS)

Left: The RAF Flying Club badge in detail. (Richard Riding)

Below: Auster J-1, G-AIGJ of the RAF Flying Club and de Havilland Technical School students in the summer of 1947. From left to right: Frank Cooper, Bill Wright, Pat Hatswell, Alistair Mackenzie, John Derbyshire, Mike Rogers, John Parkes and Derek Walker. The Auster crashed at Antwerp on 27 November 1948. (A.R. 'Pop' Bilkey)

HARD TIMES

Times were obviously hard and in July 1947 the London Aeroplane Club was brought under the wing of the de Havilland Technical School, being subsidised by the company and enabling apprentices to fly for 33 shillings per hour (£1.65), about one third of the actual cost at the time. This move hoped to bring a more active organisation, better technical facilities and fresh enthusiasm. Flt Lt Dennis A. Cather AFM was CFI and Wg Cdr J.A. Harris the club secretary and aerodrome control officer at Panshanger. The club held an Annual Ball at the Savoy and, perhaps inevitably, the 1949 AGM (after the first full year in association with the Technical School) revealed financial losses. The club listed 251 members, 1,856 hours flown and fifty-seven 'A' licences granted in 1948.

Welwyn Garden City Urban District Council restricted operations from the aerodrome during these early years, particularly as a result of noise and the danger in over-flying the growing industrial area of Welwyn Garden City and in retrospect little has changed here.

A January 1948 winter postcard, showing
LAC Tiger Moths on the north site.
(A.R. 'Pop' Bilkey)

The de Havilland DH.82A Tiger Moth is truly one of the great aircraft, tracing lineage back to the
original Moth of 1926. G-AHIZ (86533) is remarkable in being in active training since the war years. It
was built by Morris Motors at Cowley in early 1944 and issued to the RAF as PG624 to de Havilland at
Witney on 31 March 1944, apparently for trials, communications and weather flights. After the war and
storage PG624 was sold to the de Havilland Aircraft Co. and registered

G-AHIZ on 23 April 1946, being painted
in the London Aeroplane Club colours
of yellow and silver. She was flown to
Panshanger to become one of the first post-
war club aircraft. After a few mishaps and
subsequent repairs and rebuilds 'HIZ was
sold to W.F.A. 'Bill' Ison and Partners, No.22
Flying Group at Cambridge, during March
1956 and collected from Panshanger at an
agreed price of £325. In front of 'HIZ in
this 1947 shot is Mike Rogers in his Austin
Seven Special. (A.R. 'Pop' Bilkey)

On 28 August 1948 Tiger Moth
G-AHXC was flown to victory by Pat
Fillingham in the 'Tiger Moth Scratch
Race' at Lympne. In front of the aircraft
are, left to right: Alistair Mackenzie,
George Hart (chief engineer), Frank
Cobb, Roy Blay, Dave Ewer and Hilary
Bowman. (A.R. 'Pop' Bilkey)

SAAB 91a Safir, SE-BNX, owned by the
Swedish Embassy, London, based and
maintained by the London Aeroplane
Club at Panshanger, one of two Safir's
at Panshanger. This aircraft had been
delivered to the Swedish Air Force on
19 June 1947, serialled 91118 and
transferred to civil use on 22 April 1949. It
returned to the Swedish Air Force on 25
August 1952 but crashed at Tiptree, Essex,
on 13 July 1959. (A.R. 'Pop' Bilkey)

Tiger Moth G-AHIZ after a forced landing near the aerodrome in 1949 or 1950, following engine failure. Inspecting the Tiger Moth are Dennis Cather, CFI of the London Aeroplane Club from 1947–1951 and C. Martin Sharp (the pilot). The Tiger Moth was rebuilt. (A.R. 'Pop' Bilkey)

On 26 June 1948 Tiger Moth G-AITA, flown by Peter Shaw, met an unfortunate end whilst attempting to land in a field near the grounds of the Red Lion public house by the Great North Road at Ayot Green. During some solo aerobatics the engine failed causing a hasty forced landing. Peter Shaw was unhurt in the accident but the Tiger suffered terminal disfigurement. (A.R. 'Pop' Bilkey)

Improvements were made to the buildings that year, with a small hangar being taken over for overhaul and major maintenance and the club-house receiving a veranda. A Moth Minor coupe (G-AFOJ, the prototype) was handed over to the club and an example of the new Chipmunk promised for the summer of 1949. An Auster J-1 (G-AGYN), loaned by the RAF Flying Club, was used for overseas flights and the rest of the fleet now consisted of five Tigers, three Hornet Moths and a Moth Minor on loan. Concern was expressed at the AGM that petrol tax would cost the club £450 and flying rates might have to be increased.

DENNIS CATHER

Dennis Cather, the CFI from 1947 until 1951, had learned to fly pre-war with the Herts and Essex Aero Club at Broxbourne, becoming one of the youngest CFI's in the country at the time. During the hostilities he became an instructor with the Empire Air Training Scheme, located in Canada. He returned to the UK in 1944 and flew operations on Mosquito night intruders with 239 Squadron, prior to demobilisation and after a brief flourish at Herts and Essex Aero Club,

On 10 June 1950 popular radio presenter Brian Johnston was entertained by the London Aeroplane Club as part of his programme *In Town Tonight*. Instructor Don MacBeath is about to get airborne in G-AKDN. The shot is highly significant in other respects since it shows construction of the new servicing hangar in the background, which was ready for the parents' day on 1 July. (BAE SYSTEMS)

A contrast in heights from the previous picture showing Brian Johnston and Don MacBeath together at Panshanger on 10 June 1950. The race numbers on the side of the Chipmunk signify its entry in the King's Cup that year. (BAE SYSTEMS)

Broxbourne, took the job with the London Aeroplane Club. Part-time instructors at the time were Messrs Don Macbeath, Dawson and Parker, with George Hart as chief engineer.

THE TECHNICAL SCHOOL

On 1 July 1950 the Technical School held an 'at home' for parents, meeting at Astwick Manor and (in the afternoon) Panshanger, where Sir Geoffrey de Havilland presented the club, via Dennis Cather, its first Chipmunk trainer, G-AKDN. Formation flying by the club and 1 RFS aircraft opened the display and was followed by demonstration flights of the Chipmunk by Pat Fillingham, the Heron prototype (Geoffrey Pike), the Vampire with re-heat (Chris Beaumont) and Vampire aerobatics (John Derry). An array of current de Havilland types was displayed and with them the veteran Cirrus Moth G-EBLV, which is still extant and maintained at Old Warden.

On 1 July 1950 de Havilland Technical School held a prize-giving and parents' open day at Astwick Manor and Panshanger, where a flying display was laid on. The main event took place on the north site, marking the opening of the new maintenance hangar, seen in the top quarter. This hangar provided all weather protection from the elements for the London Aeroplane Club. The buildings can be clearly seen with, just left of centre, the veranda added to the clubhouse (the old 'B' flight hut). This building still exists though deeply overgrown, as does the MT building in the centre. Of further interest are the three RAF barrack huts being erected to the right of the tree line. These still stand and are in private hands. The RAF Mess sits to the left of these and is privately owned. The reason for their survival is largely due to the reacquisition of farmland by Mr C.J. Barton after the sale of the aerodrome in 1953. Eventually a large earth bank was added to separate the airfield from the farm and whilst the airfield buildings deteriorated to decay those on the farm survive.

    On the airfield can be seen the London Aeroplane Club aircraft and the latest de Havilland types; the Heron prototype, G-ALZL, a Dove, G-ALBM and a Vampire FB.52 of the Norwegian Air Force. (BAE SYSTEMS)

The day provided an ideal PR opportunity for the official handover of the first Chipmunk aircraft to the London Aeroplane Club, in fact the first to any civilian flying club. Notable people in the photograph are, from left to right: Sir Geoffrey de Havilland, T.A. Stanley (LAC Committee), Flt Lt Dennis Cather (LAC CFI) and Mr Nixon. (BAE SYSTEMS)

The Thomson Brothers (Bilston) fuel bowser used by the London Aeroplane Club and in 1950, newly painted by Shell BP for the Parents' Day on 1 July 1950. Left to right: Norman Savory, Mike Simpson (perched on top), 'Nick' Nicholson sitting on the ground and 'Pop' Bilkey. (A.R. 'Pop' Bilkey)

The Vampire FB.52 of the Royal Norwegian Air Force can be seen, together with Anson, WB462 'RCM-7' and de Havilland DH.114 Heron 1, G–ALZL at Panshanger on 1 July 1950. (BAE SYSTEMS)

Prepared for the 1951 National Air Races, scheduled for 23 June at Hatfield. Unfortunately the weather had other ideas and the races were cancelled. Standing left to right: John K. Brown, Eric Dyer, C. Martin Sharp, Dennis Cather (CFI), Tim Hilton, George Hart, John Cooper. Middle row, left to right: Jim Greathead, Ken Sapsed, Dave Hawkes. Front row, left to right: 'Pop' Bilkey, Chris Holland, Bob Kurzen, Kim Stanton. (A.R. 'Pop' Bilkey)

The first British-registered (tenth Canadian-built) Chipmunk G–AJVD was used by de Havilland for demonstrations from May 1947 and moved to Panshanger for the London Aeroplane Club in June 1951. The club was very privileged in receiving three Chipmunks around this time, though the prototype, G–AKEV, was not used regularly. Here 'JVD flies over the north site in 1951, a contrast with the shot some three years earlier showing Hornet Moth 'DKW. 'JVD was sold to J.J. Sledmore in September 1959. (BAE SYSTEMS)

The prototype de Havilland DH.114 Heron 1, G-ALZL lands at Panshanger on 16 June 1950. The Heron was in essence a scaled-up four-engine Dove, using many common components, and Geoffrey Pike had made the first flight from Hatfield on 10 May 1950. He flew the aircraft at the Parents' Open Day on 1 July. (BAE SYSTEMS)

De Havilland Canada DHC-1 Chipmunk G-AKDN was imported in August 1947 to act as a company demonstrator and duly passed to the London Aeroplane Club in July 1950. The club entered 'KDN in the *Daily Express* Air Race on 16 September 1950 from Hurn around the south soast but had to withdraw. It was flown in the King's Cup during 1951 and in May 1952, flown by Pat Fillingham, won the Goodyear Air Challenge Trophy and he became British Air Racing Champion. In 1953, flying 'KDN, he won the King's Cup. 'KDN was used by the club until it was sold in 1961. (BAE SYSETMS)

Volunteer Reserve (VR) officer and instructor with 1 RFS, Brian Hamilton, sits in the cockpit of G-AKDN during a photograph session at Panshanger on 1 September 1951. (BAE SYSTEMS)

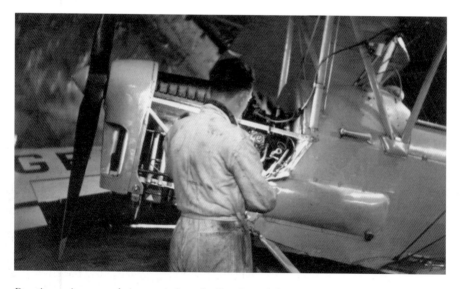

Routine maintenance being carried out by Ken Sapsed during a fifty-hour inspection on a London Aeroplane Club Tiger Moth. (A.R. 'Pop' Bilkey)

VR officers Freydis Leaf (left), Margaret Frost and instructor Brian Hamilton inspect the London Aeroplane Club Chipmunk, G-AKDN. The Chipmunk was designed and built by de Havilland's Canadian subsidiary as their first indigenous post-war design and became a successful elementary trainer. Large numbers were built to UK requirements at de Havilland's Chester facility for RAF, Royal Navy, Army and export. Its relative complexity and expense made it less attractive to cash-strapped civil flying clubs in the early years. (BAE SYSTEMS)

Mal Williams, known to most as 'Taffy', with his Riley 9 Special. After rebuilding the chassis he hand-made the complete body, doing his own panel beating and welding, from aluminium sheet. He hand-made detail fittings such as door handles, boot hinges etc. The head lamps were Avro Anson landing lights. (A.R. 'Pop' Bilkey)

The sole surviving Hucks Starter, completely restored in 1952 by the de Havilland Technical School students under the supervision of George Hart, Chief Engineer of the London Aeroplane Club. The Ford Model 'T'-based vehicle is still in use with the Shuttleworth Trust at Old Warden. (A.R. 'Pop' Bilkey)

During 1950 the club received another Chipmunk in the form of the prototype G-AKEV but, being frequently unserviceable having been a test bed, was withdrawn from use by January 1951. Later, the remains were transported to Digswell for use by David Carnegie.

De Havilland used the space at Panshanger for aircraft storage during the 1950s. Frustrated cancellations of orders for the de Havilland Dove resulted in several being stored in the north site blister hangars from early in 1951. These included G-AMXS, which was re-registered in Venezuela in 1953 but remained at Panshanger for while longer.

By 1954 the dismantled de Havilland Mosquito prototype W4050 was stored at Panshanger, probably in the 69' 'B' Flight blister hangar. There it remained until being moved to storage in the Hatfield area (Fiddlebridge) following the acquisition of the aerodrome operations by Nat Somers. The Mosquito led a charmed life, escaping the accountants and axe men until stored and displayed from 1959 in its own hangar at Salisbury Hall, London Colney where it had been built. This has preserved the aircraft for all time, eventually allowing its display at the Mosquito Aircraft Museum.

A NEW HANGAR

A new blister hangar was constructed on the north side during 1950 to undertake maintenance and engineering work throughout the year. This hangar faced east–west with a brick workshop on the west-facing end for a better working environment and was situated behind the London Aeroplane Club hangars.

When the club vacated the northern area in 1953, the 'new' hangar was used by Mr Barton of Warrengate Farm for pig rearing and hay storage. It was demolished during the 1990s after vandalism and fire damage.

By 1952 the club fleet grew by one Chipmunk (G-AJVD) and Sqdn Ldr Don Macbeath took over as the CFI on 1 January after Dennis Cather left the country to join the Toronto Flying Club and later the Canadian Board of Transport. 'At home' days, 'Breakfast Patrols' and general flying meetings held sway throughout 1952 and the club flew 2,414 hours (381 more than 1951) with training assisted by five part-time instructors. Half the 194 new members that year were de Havilland employees taking advantage of the cheap flying. Thirteen ATC cadets of 22 attached to the club, following the award of flying scholarships, successfully completed their PPL course.

TRAGEDY

On 28 June 1952 the club lost one of the Tiger Moths, G-AHXC, in a fatal crash in Hatfield Park. The pilot, Charles Woosnam, was flying solo and eyewitnesses (including an entire Boy Scout camp) suggested that engine trouble had caused an attempted forced landing. Investigation revealed the aircraft stalled at too low a level for the pilot to recover.

Pat Fillingham talks with aerodrome engineer George Hart about the forthcoming South Coast *Daily Express* Air Race held on 16 September 1950. Pat flew G-AFOJ to Hurn on 14 September after last-minute preparations; however, he finished tenth overall and third in class. (BAE SYSTEMS)

On 25 July 1953, around the time the airfield's future was in the balance following the auction of the Panshanger estate, the London Aeroplane Club held a National Air Touring Competition. This was a test of navigation skill in plotting and flying involving a variety of visiting aircraft to the aerodrome. Here Moth Minor, G-AFPN, named 'Escape', prepares to depart at an allotted time. (BAE SYSTEMS)

A much larger de Havilland type prepares for the same exercise. At this time Dove 1, G-AJGT, was owned by the manufacturers and retained for engine trials through the 1950s and 1960s, being Leavesden-based with Bristol Siddeley Engines from 1961. (BAE SYSTEMS)

Top: On 17 July 1952 the London Aeroplane Club lines up its aircraft for a photo shoot and included significant others in the frame. The Messenger G-AGPX was owned by David 'Angus' Carnegie, chairman of Carnegie Chemicals in Welwyn Garden City. The Saab 91A Safir ('91123') was an early Swedish Air Force example, used by de Havilland for Gipsy Major engine trials and based at Panshanger and Hatfield. In the background is the area now known as Moneyhole Lane Park whilst the blister hangar in the distance was being used by the Gliding School. (BAE SYSTEMS)

Above: This shot of G-AHXC was taken at Panshanger in 1946. The Tiger Moth served as T6745 with 29 EFTS and was civilian registered on 30 April 1946, joining the London Aeroplane Club in June that year. In August 1948 'HXC was entered for the Air Races held at Lympne, flown by Pat Fillingham, which he duly won at an average speed of 86mph. The following year C. Martin Sharpe planned to fly 'HXC in the National Air Races at Elmdon but prior to the race it was hit by another Tiger at Panshanger. On 28 June 1952 Charles Woosnam was flying solo over Hatfield Park and crashed with fatal results. (Richard Riding)

Opposite above: One of the oldest surviving Moths, G-EBLV, is owned by British Aerospace and kept in flying condition with the Shuttleworth Trust at Old Warden, Bedfordshire. On 1 July 1950 she was shown at Panshanger following refurbishment by de Havilland and in 1953 was given a temporary certificate of airworthiness to take part in the Festival of Flight celebrations to mark the fiftieth anniversary of man-powered flight. A full restoration commenced later. This view is dated 21 June 1958, taken during the Panshanger flying display. (MAP)

Opposite below: Actually taken on 15 October 1953 following the closure of the Reserve Flying Schools, the former military south site was used by the London Aeroplane Club. This photograph was used for the Christmas edition of the *de Havilland Gazette* house magazine but is significant in other respects since the airfield was then in private hands. Chipmunk G-AKDN is inundated with well-wishers. (BAE SYSTEMS)

CIRRUS MOTH

It was also noted that the club continued to maintain the vintage de Havilland-owned Moth, G-EBLV under supervision of the technical school. The aircraft was permitted to fly for the Festival of Flight in 1953 but afterwards it was withdrawn for a full overhaul.

MOVE TO THE SOUTH SITE

The closure of the RFS during 1953 and the subsequent winding down of the south side of the aerodrome facilities jeopardised the future support of the club by de Havilland but they continued nonetheless. In June 1953 Pat Fillingham, flying a club Chipmunk (G-AKDN), won the King's Cup air race and 162 new members joined up to the end of the year. 3,172 hours were flown, forty-one new PPLs were obtained and much overseas flying was undertaken. Such were the excellent standards of maintenance undertaken by George Hart that the club's Tigers flew up to eight hours each day during the summer. The engineering expertise was such that a local modification of the de Havilland Moth Minor to a more comfortable coupe variant was approved and at least two former 'open cockpit' aircraft altered accordingly.

10

Panshanger 1953

By 1953 the future of the aerodrome was now a cause for concern as plans went ahead for the sale of the Panshanger estate, its attendant farms and land. The large house and gardens occupied a sizeable landscaped area to the east of the aerodrome boundary, across Panshanger Lane. Since the death of the heirs to the Cowper family and their relations, the house had fallen into disrepair. The auction of the house, land and farms went ahead on 15 July 1953 and raised a great deal of public interest. The land occupied by the aerodrome, its RAF buildings, hangars and air-raid facilities were covered under Lots 2, 5, 6 and 12 of the sale brochure. This was listed as land under Air Ministry requisition from Mr C.J. Barton of Warrengate Farm and Marden Dairy Farm (Lot 2), Tewinbury Farm (Lot 5), Attimore Hall Farm and land (Lot 6) and woodlands near Cole Green (Henry Wood Lot 12). Suffice it is to say the largest area of concern, the arable land used for the runways and supporting the aerodrome buildings, came under Warrengate and Marden Farms control (169 acres). (Appendix 5).

During the auction Lot 2 reached £23,500 but was withdrawn from the sale. Attimore Hall Farm was sold for £12,500 to the tenant, Mr Crawford, and its land (Lot 6) acquired by the Welwyn Garden City Development Corporation for future housing (a designated area order). The woodlands went to Mr Robert Wallace of Inns & Co. gravel merchants for future gravel extraction. The house, now dilapidated, was acquired for £17,750 by a demolition contractor, Mr Richard Ashton, and was later levelled to the ground.

WELWYN GARDEN CITY EXPANSION

There is no doubt the land occupied by the aerodrome was of great interest to controllers of the development of Welwyn Garden City since the Urban District Council had plans for eastern expansion of the town through the second half of the century. The council had made efforts to control the use of the aerodrome, including requests to the Air Ministry and Ministry of Town & Country Planning demanding closure from as far back as July 1948. These stemmed from complaints about noise and pollution to the dangers from aircraft flying close to the growing industrial area on the east of the town. Early plans (1949) for expansion of housing in what later became Panshanger estate were used as the main thrust towards closing the aerodrome for good. An agreement to continue operation of the Reserve School and civil flying until 30 June 1950 was made with the council adamant that reviews after this would take place every six months. Conversely the Air Ministry wished to retain the aerodrome for training purposes and were concerned the limitations would harm recruiting and moral.

The current state of affairs, letters in the press and so on, concerning noise pollution from the aerodrome are no different to those of 1950! The growing concern about closure reached the press in 1952 and the local business community issued support for its retention claiming it performed a valuable service for companies. This was a result of a still-born decision by the London Aeroplane Club to move to Leavesden Aerodrome. WGCUDC retorted there was not the slightest chance the aerodrome would be retained (31 December 1952).

By 15 January 1953 Humbert & Flint were given instructions to dispose of the estate and WGC Corporation expressed immediate interest in purchasing the aerodrome and approached the Ministry of Housing and Local Government. In this way the council would control the aerodrome and its development. It was obvious the incumbent owners, de Havilland Aircraft Co. and the London Aeroplane Club, preferred to retain ownership and a meeting was arranged with the various parties at Nast Hyde in March 1953.

The main topic concerning de Havilland was the outline plan for housing development, since it would impose a severe restriction on the aerodrome and inevitably lead to closure. The Corporation outlined the need for town expansion from 36,000 to 50,000 people, notably in no small part a result of de Havilland increasing their work force.

The Corporation was desperate to start work on the land (initially 130 acres to the west of the aerodrome) as soon as possible since finances from the Treasury would not be available unless this could be carried out rapidly. Robert Wallace of Inns & Co., the gravel extractors, were tasked with carrying out preparatory work north of Attimore Hall Farm since gravel extraction brought quick profit.

Inns & Co., however, could not find significant gravel in this area, which was a blow to the Corporation. The Corporation continued in the main development of the Haldens and Black Fan (Panshanger) area (750 acres) and left the decision to purchase the aerodrome outright from the sale of the estate to de Havilland themselves.

The Miles Messenger was designed as a four-seat light liaison aircraft for the Army and post-war adapted readily to civilian life. Under Class 'B' marks as U-0273, this Messenger 2B (6266) was a three-seat variant used as a Cirrus Major test-bed by Blackburn Aircraft from June 1945. Registered G-AGPX with a C of A issued on 6 November 1945, it was sold to Angus D.M.B. Carnegie (owner of Carnegie Chemicals) at Panshanger, who had been taught to fly there by Dennis Cather. His sons later learned to fly and naturally used the Messenger. Carnegie sold the aircraft to P.J. Butterfield in 1958, the Messenger staying at Panshanger for a while until moving to Stapleford Tawney where it was withdrawn from use in March 1962. (APN)

By 25 June 1953 Longmores (de Havilland solicitors) requested from the Corporation permanent closure of Moneyhole Lane, which previously ran through the centre of the aerodrome but had been stopped up in 1945 under Defence Regulation 16. The sale of the estate went ahead and the Corporation missed out on further land acquisition due to some internal reluctance to support the purchase.

Within a year de Havilland Aircraft Co. had pulled out of continued financial support for London Aeroplane Club and left its operation to Nat Somers.

NAT SOMERS

By the middle of 1953 continued support of the club by the de Havilland Co. was in jeopardy and the decision made to sell the aerodrome and club to private hands. The land occupied by the aerodrome and its buildings was sold to Mr John Nathaniel (Nat) Somers who acquired rights to the London Aeroplane Club from de Havilland at the same time. Nat Somers was well known in aviation circles and as a highly successful air-racing pilot had won the prestigious King's Cup on 30 July 1949 flying his Miles Gemini 3, G-AKDC.

Nat was one of six pilots who in 1949 formed the unofficial 'Throttle-Benders Union' of air-racing pilots who had won at least one major race.

Nat Somers was born in June 1909 and learned to fly at Ford in 1936. He transferred to Brooklands Aviation later and joined the Royal Air Force as an instructor with 6 EFTS at Sywell. He was awarded the Air Force Cross in April 1944 for distinguished service with elementary flying training. On 10 December 1942 he was posted to Holwell Hyde from 6 EFTS,

Nat Somers acquired Miles Gemini 3 G-AKDC on 9 May 1949, based initially at Elstree and, by June 1954, Panshanger. It was modified for his highly successful foray into air racing, hugely popular in the UK during the 1950s. The 'throttle-benders union' of air-racing pilots used a number of tactics to hoodwink the marshals and handicappers. It was not unknown for a complete engine change to be carried out between heats and the race. 'KDC was the prototype series 3 having 145hp Gipsy Major 1C engines and was famous as the winning aircraft in the 1949 King's Cup Air Race. It was sold to Wescol Engineering at Yeadon on 9 March 1956. (Richard Riding)

Sywell, for three weeks' night-flying instructor's duties, followed by a return to the aerodrome on 13 June 1945 as a flying instructor.

After Air Force service he built up several companies, including J.N. Somers Ltd of Acton and Maidenhead, which produced plugs and sockets for aircraft and ground equipment. Other companies included Somers Lamps Ltd.

Air racing was hugely popular during the 1950s and Nat Somers flew his modified Miles Gemini to great success. During the 1950 King's Cup with unfavourable handicapping he finished sixteenth but broke the world 100km closed-circuit record for his class, at 168.44mph. He came second that year in the Goodyear Trophy race. In May 1953 he purchased the racing Percival Mew Gull, G-AEXF, which had been rebuilt by Doug Bianchi at Booker, and raced it in the Kemsley Trophy race at Southend. The Mew Gull was sold to Fred Dunkerley at Barton in September 1954. In 1953 he won the Siddeley Challenge Trophy, the following year the Kemsley Challenge Trophy, at 174.5mph and in 1955 the Goodyear Trophy again. He was proclaimed British Air Racing Champion that year too.

SOMERS-KENDALL AIRCRAFT

1954 saw Nat Somers initiate the high-profile Somers-Kendall Aircraft Co. Hugh Kendall designed the pretty two-seat Somers-Kendall SK.1 of all-wood construction and jet-powered for Nat Somers to compete in the British Air-Racing formula during 1956. One 330lb thrust Turbomeca Palas turbojet was sufficient to enable the aircraft to reach 322mph. The aircraft was constructed at Woodley, Berkshire, during 1954–55 and registered G-AOBG. No air racing was possible during 1956 due to problems with the aircraft. On 5 May 1956 Hugh Kendall had to retract the undercarriage to prevent over-running the runway at Hatfield after the engine failed on take-off. Following a turbine failure in the air on 11 July 1957 the pretty SK-1 was stored at Cranfield and never flown again.

The SK-1 still exists, however, and is currently stored dismantled at Breighton, East Yorkshire, under the protection of the 'Real Aeroplane Company'.

In 1956 Nat Somers flew the Chipmunk, G-AKDN, to victory in the National Air Races at Yeadon, winning the Osram Cup. In addition to the ownership of Panshanger Nat Somers purchased Southampton Airport from the City Council in 1961 and is noted as the person responsible for developing the airport into a major regional presence. Somers sold the airport in November 1988 to Peter de Savary's company, Highland Investments, for £55 million. Up to his death Nat Somers continued to fly and was often in command of the Tower House Consultants Falcon 900B, based at Southampton or Jersey, where he lived.

Through his role as a liveryman with the Guild of Airline Pilot's and Navigators (GAPAN) his widow, Phyllis, made a generous bequest for an award to a suitable applicant towards the Airline Transport Pilot Licence. This is known as the J.N. Somers Award in recognition of his service.

Nat Somers died on 12 March 1998 in Jersey, aged eighty-eight years.

11

Panshanger Aerodrome Under New Ownership

Under the new ownership the London Aeroplane Club continued, however, and began to re-equip, selling two Tiger Moths (G-AHUB and G-AHXB) to New Zealand in May 1954. These were exported to Balclutha via Blakes Wharf, Fulham, on board the SS *Laurentian Forest* and became ZK-BFM and ZK-BFL respectively.

The future of the club was still subject to media attention but a report in the *Evening News* of 28 July 1954 announced that Panshanger Aerodrome had a reprieve from the WGC Council and would be allowed to operate under restrictions. These included the use of piston-engine light aircraft only using defined funnels for approach and landing. At this time the aerodrome used a four-runway pattern, basically similar to the Air Ministry map. The housing development to the west of the aerodrome would restrict this considerably over the years.

Around 1954 the club relocated to the south side of the aerodrome, taking over the vacated RFS hangars and buildings (including the RAF admin block) and changed its name slightly to the North London Aero Club, being run by E.A. Gilbert. Two aircraft were acquired during 1955, G-AHHN, an Auster Autocrat and G-AHSD, a Taylorcraft Plus D, with the club's CFI being Mr Maile. The club's former location on the north side of the aerodrome gradually fell into disrepair though one of the larger Miskin blister hangars remains, albeit as a skeletal shell. The North London Aero Club acquired additional Taylorcraft Plus D, G-AFZI and G-AHVR. On 28 October 1956 'HVR force-landed at Potters Bar after the engine failed. It was ferried back to Panshanger by road for repair. Almost a year later (26 October 1957) 'FZI was involved in a force-landing at Hitchin after the pilot became lost. Minor damage resulted. The club survived until 1959.

In October 1955 Fisons Airwork, a company involved in crop spraying, approached the Corporation seeking thirty houses for employees engaged in helicopter works at Panshanger. Whilst the council supported the use of passenger operations from the aerodrome it did not like the idea of industrial undertakings and the request was turned down. Fisons moved elsewhere.

In November 1955 a revised plan for the future development of the Panshanger area was unveiled by the Architects for the Corporation under Louis de Soissons involving large areas of land set aside for playing fields. A large school was planned (the High School/Attimore Hall School) for the area east of Herns Lane near Grubs Barn. It appears that the London Aeroplane Club had plans to develop the use of the aerodrome as well, though still nominally under the confines of the restriction order of 1948. In 1956, now three years on from the aerodrome being sold, the closure and redirection of Moneyhole Lane was still not agreed and it would take a further three years until the new footpath opened.

After wartime service as NL763 this Tiger Moth was civilianised and registered G-AHUB on 6 June 1946 for the Cambridge Aero Club. It was sold to the London Aeroplane Club on 26 July 1948 and is seen at Panshanger around this time with instructor Don Macbeath about to take young Jim Mead airborne for a photographic sortie. G-AHUB was sold in New Zealand as ZK-BFM on 17 March 1954 and crated at Blakes Wharf, London for shipping via the SS *Laurentian Forest*. It arrived in New Zealand on 25 May 1954. (Jim Mead)

This Auster J-1 Autocrat G-AHHN arrived at Panshanger in December 1955 registered to the North London Aero Club. It is seen here around 1961 outside the rather battered canvas frontage of the maintenance blister hangar on the south site, contrasting with the earlier photographs. The Auster departed for Trans Jordan (Jordan) in June 1965 and was re-registered JY-GYT. (APN)

This Tiger Moth was built by Morris Motors, Cowley, and entered service with the Royal Air Force as T5978 joining the Service Ferry Pilots Pool. Later it was used by Army Cooperation Command Communications Flight and 245 Squadron RAF. It was sold in May 1946 and became G-AHXB on 27 June 1946 for the London Aeroplane Club at Panshanger. It served for eight years until it was sold in New Zealand in March 1954, with sister G-AHUB, becoming ZK-BFL. She was crated and despatched via Blakes Wharf, London, being shipped on 25 May 1954. In the photograph Jim Mead sits in the front cockpit with Dennis Cather, the CFI, in the rear. Jim became well known as a sports photographer as well as for his aviation shots. He is credited with photographing the dramatic last moments of an English Electric Lightning at Hatfield following an engine fire, with pilot George Aird safely ejecting moments before the aircraft plunged to the ground. (Jim Mead)

C.H. Hammer/North London Aeroplane Club acquired this Taylorcraft Plus D, G-AHSD, in December 1955 for flying training, the CFI at the time being Mr Maile. The photograph is dated 1961 and 'HSD was sold in June 1966. (NA3T/ATPH Transportphotos)

Built by Percival at Luton and delivered to the RAF as DX240 this Proctor served with 1 Signals School and the Bristol Wireless Flight prior to storage. It was sold on 21 February 1949, becoming G-ALIT with Wolverhampton Flying Schools Ltd initially and Midland Aeroplane Club in June 1952. It moved to Panshanger around August 1955 with new owner M. Niblett. On 17 May 1956 Beverley Snook landed at Panshanger and ran into a ditch, severely damaging the aircraft. 'LIT was withdrawn from use and parked between two blister hangars on the south site until burnt later. Beverley Snook was chairman of Transglobal Aviation Supply and noted for the import of Spitfire IX, OO-ARE, used in the 1961 London to Cardiff Air Race. (Maurice Freeman)

Registered to G.H.M.S. Peverel in July 1952, this Taylorcraft Plus D, G-AHVR, was later operated by the North London Aeroplane Club. Taylorcraft Aeroplanes had been formed in November 1938 to build under licence Taylor Young monoplanes. The Plus D was powered by a 90hp Blackburn Cirrus Minor engine and formed the basis of the successful Auster J-1 design. On 28 October 1956 'HVR force-landed at Potters Bar after the engine failed. It was ferried back to Panshanger by road for repair and used until sold in February 1962 following replacement by newer types. (MAP)

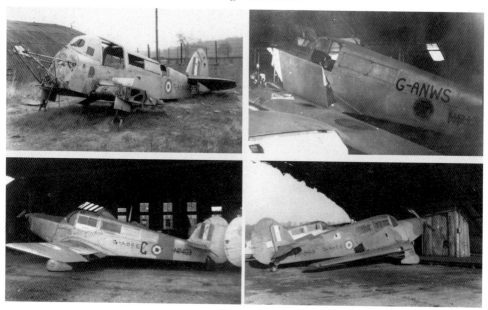

Over the winter of 1954/55 many surplus Percival Proctor 4s were sold by the RAF. A total of fourteen was purchased by Aerocontracts and Continental Aircraft Services for conversion to civil use at Panshanger and at least twelve recorded at one time. All were registered with crudely painted serials and languished in the large Miskin blister hangar on the north site and a storage area between the blister hangars on the south site. The venture failed and all were scrapped during 1957, followed by a rather splendid Guy Fawkes' Night that November. Parts of these aircraft were unearthed in the early 1990s. (APN)

The Chipmunk was an all-metal, two-seat tandem trainer designed in Canada to replace the Tiger Moth. Initially it was a little expensive for civilian flying clubs but after a few years service surplus examples came onto the UK market. This Chipmunk was the 100th built, unusual in having no RAF service history. It was registered on 28 December 1949 as G-ALWB to de Havilland Aircraft for UK demonstrations, based at Hatfield and Panshanger. In 1951 Pat Fillingham won the Goodyear Trophy Race flying G-ALWB at an average speed of 142mph. In August 1956. it was sold in Austria as OE-ABC for personal use of DH representative, Nikolaus Eltz. It returned to the UK in April 1961 as G-ALWB for the London Aeroplane Club at Panshanger, the photograph taken around this time. In April 1963 it was sold to the Lebanese Army along with a number of refurbished Chipmunks but held in reserve. It returned to Panshanger in June 1971 with new owners K.C. Keegan & Ptnrs of Keegan Aviation but during 1972 moved to Stansted. (MAP)

Robinson Redwing, G-ABNX, was built during March 1932 by Redwing Aircraft Ltd of Blue Barns Aerodrome, Colchester. The Redwing was a two-seat, side-by-side, touring aircraft built in limited numbers. 'BNX is the sole survivor and had seen only a few owners before being stored by V. Mitchell at Panshanger from 1953 until the late 1950s, moving to Heath End, near Farnham. From here it was acquired in December 1959 by John Pothecary and E.H. Gould and restored to fly at Christchurch. (Maurice Freeman)

Derek R.C.B. de Sarigny at Panshanger on 21 June 1958, the CFI of the North London Aero Club at the time. Derek Barrois de Sarigny was born in Johannesburg in 1909 and joined the RAF in 1930. By 1940 he was a Flying Instructor at RAF Brize Norton and reached the rank of Squadron Leader. Post-war he became closely associated with Panshanger and the variety of flying clubs that sprouted and often failed. (AEROPLANE MONTHLY/ www.aeroplanemonthly.com)

Registered originally as N8590D this Piper PA-18A Super Cub was the first
example to be registered in the UK. G-APKB was bought by Sheriff Grain Dryers
Ltd at Panshanger and moved to Croydon on 28 February 1958 before returning
with Farmair on 21 April 1958. It is seen on 21 June 1958 during the Panshanger
Air Display. The torn canvas of the maintenance hangar is noteworthy by this time.
(*AEROPLANE MONTHLY*/www.aeroplanemonthly.com)

*Welwyn & Hatfield
Times* advertisement
for the Midsummer
Air Display of 21 June
1958. (*Welwyn Hatfield
Times*)

The new route runs today along the western edge of the aerodrome, cutting through the Panshanger housing estate. The northern route heads down the hill to the B1000. The path was formally agreed in August 1959.

During the latter part of the decade the British private and club-flying scene began to emerge after a difficult financial period. Panshanger became a haven for the private flier and small business concern with many well-known personalities and companies setting up there. Some enterprises failed, however; for several years the sight of many Percival Proctors languishing on the north side of the aerodrome was testament to a failed attempt to convert these ex-RAF radio trainers and communication aircraft for civilian use. At least twelve arrived during 1955 but most were scrapped and burned on Guy Fawkes' Night 1957. Their remains were still being unearthed forty years later.

The London Aeroplane Club held an air display at Panshanger on 21 June 1958 with the Tiger Club visiting from Redhill. An RAF Vampire T.11 XE831 gave a sprightly display.

HERTFORDSHIRE POLICE

Among several small flying groups formed at Panshanger in the 1950s was the Hertfordshire Police Flying Club. Established on 15 September 1956, the small group purchased a single Tiger Moth, G-ANOH, from the London Aeroplane Club and refurbished it for training, operating out of the Miskin Extra-Over blister hangar on the north side, where 1 RFS Ansons had been located. Several police employees gained their PPL over the next few years and the Tiger was used for aerial photography and police searches. Gradually membership fell away and the club closed in 1960, the Tiger Moth joining the Luton Flying Club.

AERIAL AGRICULTURE

The beginnings of aerial agriculture (crop-spraying) had their roots at Panshanger with several small companies pioneering the industry by modifying the venerable Tiger Moth to carry insecticide or fertilisers in a hopper that replaced the front cockpit. Spray & Win Ltd and Agricultural & Aviation Ltd were two operations set up by ex-service pilots in the 1950s but although the techniques were sound the companies folded. Spray & Win was formed in 1950 by James Holland, an American who served with the RCAF during the war. The Tiger Moth was modified severely, with the front cockpit removed and a large hopper with 500lb capacity fitted in its place. Chemicals would exit the hopper into a venturi-shaped sprayer and be distributed evenly into the aircraft's slipstream and onto the field below. Operating costs were claimed to be £3 per hour and in that time the Tiger Moth could dust 100 acres. Rollason's at Croydon performed the conversion and were heavily involved in converting Tiger Moths for civilian use at the time. The low initial cost of the aircraft was quite attractive too, since a war-weary Tiger could be bought for as little as £50.

Opposite below: Another of the many Tiger Moths sold into civilian use in the 1950s, G-ANOH was one of four purchased in February 1954 by the London Aeroplane Club. G-ANOG and G-ANOI were stripped for spares and the author remembers 'NOG being derelict in one of the blister hangars during the late 1960s. It was buried in land sold for housing several years later. 'NOH was sold to the Hertfordshire Police Flying Club in August 1956 and used for PPL training and police use until membership fell away. It was sold to the Luton Flying Club in April 1960. (1166 (WGC) Squadron Air Training Corps)

Above: A close-up of Tiger Moth G-AKXG showing the crude operating lever for the hopper flap on the port side of the fuselage. The pilot has very little protection and later conversions of the Tiger Moth employed a much larger 'Perspex' screen. The toll on the airframe was immense through stress, frequent damage and corrosion from the chemicals. It would be expected that the pilot complained as well. (BAE SYSTEMS)

AGRICULTURAL AVIATION CO.

Agricultural & Aviation was formed in early 1958 by Danny Speck at Chirnside, near Duns, Berwickshire using, initially, a converted Tiger Moth G-ANNI for spraying and dusting. Arthur W.J.G. Ord-Hume was chief engineer, Roy Matthews the pilot and Edwin Howey the company secretary. A second Tiger, G-AOXX, was acquired and modified for agricultural use using a Britten-Norman hopper and pump. Later in the year Danny purchased the stores (four huts) and large blister hangar on the north site, formerly occupied by the London Aeroplane Club and 1 RFS, for the princely sum of £750. A third Tiger, G-ANCZ, joined the fleet at this time but on 16 January 1959 Tom Cahill, a new pilot, force-landed the aircraft in a field 300 yards from the aerodrome perimeter following engine failure.

By October 1958 the Agricultural Aviation Co. was running seven Tiger Moths and one Dragon Rapide from Panshanger (acquired from Hants & Sussex Aviation for crew transport). Their expertise in the conversion of Tiger Moths for aerial agriculture met with the approval of the Air Registration Board and they were allotted a Class 'B' registration, G-44-*, to be applied to their aircraft for test-flying purposes but there is some doubt as to this registration sequence being used. De Havilland was interested in using the Chipmunk trainer in the lucrative market and supplied the Mk.23 prototype crop sprayer, G-APMN, to Panshanger in June 1958 for Agricultural Aviation to improve the dusting and spraying equipment. Unfortunately the aircraft was written-off in Lincolnshire a month later and replaced by G-APOS, delivered to Panshanger by Geoffrey Pike. Despite being damaged during test flights after a pump exploded, Agricultural Aviation sorted the design. During this period de Havilland became interested in a purpose-built crop sprayer and separately Westland Helicopters supplied a S.51 Widgeon helicopter to Panshanger (G-ANLW) for possible conversion. At Southend vast RAF surplus stocks of Percival Prentice trainers, acquired by Aviation Traders, were assessed for conversion to affordable crop sprayers but this came to nothing. The burgeoning company was destined for only brief success and folded in late 1959 when bank loans were called in. Most aircraft were repossessed leaving the hulk of 'NCZ and a proposed Tiger Moth crop-sprayer with fabric removed from the rear fuselage, forlorn in the blister hangar.

Agricultural aviation pioneer, Bill Bowker, took the techniques learned from the Agricultural Aviation enterprise and relocated to a small airstrip at Rush Green, near Hitchin, Herts. Here he converted Tiger Moth and later Chipmunk aircraft as part of the successful Farm Aviation concern. These highly modified aircraft, notably Chipmunk G-APOS, the second prototype Mk.23, were operated around the Panshanger area during the top dressing seasons.

During the early 1960s Farmair set up another agricultural concern using the Piper Super Cub for crop-spraying and its aircraft were distributed between Bournemouth and remote locations.

Opposite below: After the end of the war many hundreds of surplus Tiger Moths were made available to fledgling flying clubs starved of training aircraft and strapped for cash. As little as £50 would guarantee a Tiger Moth though some overhaul and conversion to civilian use was required. This Tiger Moth served the war as T6105 as a conversion trainer with 60 OTU, Northolt Station Flight, 61 OTU and 657 Squadron (Army). It was sold on 29 April 1948 to the Surrey Financial Trust and registered G-AKXG, being overhauled by Rollason's in June 1948. In June 1950 'KXG was sold to Spray & Win Ltd and converted for crop-spraying. On 10 July 1950 a crop-spraying demonstration was held at Panshanger with a variety of aircraft, including an early de Havilland Canada Beaver, as well as the Tiger Moth. 'KXG was sold in Australia in March 1955, becoming VH-KYA. Another crop-spraying company, Agricultural & Aviation Ltd, was set up at Panshanger during 1958, again using the trusty (and cheap) Tiger Moth. The company pioneered engineering conversions on six Tiger Moths prior to setting up another operation at Rush Green, near Hitchin where de Havilland Technical School apprentice Bill Bowker formed Farm Aviation. (BAE SYSTEMS)

Top: De Havilland Tiger Moth G-AIZF saw wartime service as T7169 and was demobbed and sold to Marshalls Flying School Ltd at Teversham on 23 December 1946. It moved to the Midland Bank Flying Club in September 1948. The complex canopy arrangement seen here was added by H.M. Woodhams at Baginton during 1950. Later in the decade 'IZF was at Panshanger with the Aviron Flying Group prior to being sold to Agricultural & Aviation at Panshanger and converted for crop spraying. It moved to Farm Aviation at Rush Green, near Hitchin in September 1960. (APN)

Middle: Registered December 1947 to Gordon White & Co. Ltd, Miles M.38 Messenger 2A G-AKKC is seen at Panshanger around 1950, prior to moving to Burnaston for Derby Aviation by September 1955. It returned a month later for use by the Carnegie Flying Group until sold to E. Lloyd-Jones at White Waltham in 1959. (APN)

Bottom: Serving the war as T6818 with 21 EFTS and Aston Down this Tiger Moth was one of a large batch sold to civilian use in 1953. Registered December 1953 as G-ANKT, it was sold to R.E. Webb in May 1956 and Aviron Ltd in July 1957 and is seen at Panshanger around this time. After a couple of years it was sold on and is now owned by the Shuttleworth Collection at Old Warden, maintained in excellent condition. (David Bray)

12

The Sixties

TRAGEDY AND CLOSURE

On 4 March 1959 a Miles Gemini 1A, G-AJEX, lost a propeller from the starboard engine after the crankshaft failed just after take-off from Panshanger. The aircraft stalled and dived into the ground, hitting a tree near to the grounds of the high school, the aircraft being destroyed by fire. The pilot, Leslie O'Connor of the London Aeroplane Club, was killed and due to the seriousness of the incident the story made the headlines in the local newspaper.

1959 marked a watershed for the aerodrome with the failure of Agricultural Aviation on the north site being swiftly followed by the collapse of the North London Aeroplane Club at the end of the year. The club chairman, E.A. Gilbert, formerly residing on the aerodrome in a caravan, moved away to Foulsham and the aerodrome, now without a licensee, closed for training. This was, however, a temporary issue as the aerodrome owner sought to improve and expand the facilities by inviting secure commercial operations.

THE EXPANSION PLANS

As mentioned earlier, the London Aeroplane Club had made plans for increased use of the aerodrome, bringing in revenue to provide a going concern. The WGCUDC and Hertfordshire County Council were concerned that any development was incompatible with the town's future development. In June 1959 the London Aeroplane Club had made proposals for charter companies to use the aerodrome and to provide, service and maintain, a large new hangar. Hertfordshire County Council reluctantly allowed the construction of the hangar but subject to the aerodrome being kept under its restriction order.

This seemed to be a stumbling point, since aerodrome expansion would always conflict with the expansion of the town. Internal support within WGC and Hatfield Council provided significant evidence of the town's industry being influenced by the aerodrome's existence. It was indicated that Smith Kline French (SKF) were influenced to move to WGC because of the aerodrome and in those days, June 1959, ICI were regularly flying personnel from Hatfield to Teeside and would have welcomed Panshanger being developed into a more attractive proposition for these flights.

Louis de Soissons issued future plans for the Panshanger estate in July 1959, stating that 231 acres of the aerodrome would not be developed for housing and should be regarded as

Green Belt or Special Restraint. There were further restrictions on the use of the aerodrome, however: mainly the required closure of two of the four runways, allowing only the north–south and a redirected east–west to remain. This met with approval of the London Aeroplane Club since the new hangar would have required runway re-siting anyway. De Soissons was adamant that Panshanger should not expand into commercial operations since larger aircraft would undoubtedly add to noise and danger.

Owned by Eric Thurston of Thurston Aviation, operated by Morley Aviation and officially based at Stapleford Tawney, this Miles Gemini 1A, G-AJEX, was used by the North London Aero Club for twin-engine training. On 4 March 1959 Leslie O'Connor, the club secretary, operated his first solo flight. Sadly just after take-off a loud 'bang' was heard as the starboard engine crankshaft failed and the propeller came away. Unable to control the aircraft the pilot crashed into a tree on the sports grounds of the high school and was killed instantly. The aircraft burnt out. The photograph shows the Gemini in a previous guise with BCI Airways. (Richard Riding)

First registered on 7 December 1945 and owned by Adams Motor Services, this Auster J-1 Autocrat, G-AGVG, is seen at Panshanger in 1961 when owned by J.W. Steele. It was sold to Brooklands Aviation at Sywell in March 1966. (NA3T/ATPH Transportphotos)

Built at Hatfield in 1935 and registered G-ADLV on 12 August that year, this Tiger Moth saw service as BB750 with various EFTS and RFS post-war before being sold on 17 May 1956 as G-AORA to the Luton Flying Club. It moved to Panshanger in December 1956 registered to W.L.M. O'Connor of the North London Aero Club and was used until sold to Rollason Aircraft & Engines in April 1963. The hangar under construction behind the aircraft dates this photograph to late 1958, early 1959. (APN)

AIRWORK SERVICES AND CESSNA

London Aeroplane Club obtained permission for the new hangar and during 1960, on behalf of Airwork Services Ltd, erected the large T2 hangar which still dominates the aerodrome skyline on the south side of the aerodrome. Airwork Services had been based temporarily at Booker after relocating from Blackbushe prior to the completion of the hangar. The plan was for Airwork to complete imported Cessna aircraft delivered as crated kits via Seaboard World Airlines Lockheed Super Constellation freighters into London Heathrow Airport, test fly, sell and maintain them from the modern facilities.

As the *Welwyn Times* noted on 15 July 1960:

> Panshanger Aerodrome is being refitted with the idea of making it a centre for business flying in this part of the country. A hangar of considerable dimensions is being erected, and existing buildings, including the control tower have been renovated.

The aerodrome operated under the control of the London Aeroplane Club and the manager at this time was Mr Maurice Imray, former chairman of the Popular Flying Association. On 23 July 1960 an air display was held at Panshanger to mark the start of the Cessna franchise.

The Cessna Aircraft Co., based in Wichita, Kansas, along with Piper and Beechcraft in the USA, post-war produced a large range of modern training, club and touring aircraft to satisfy the huge domestic demand. The UK aircraft industry was never to achieve its pre-war status and some of the indigenous manufacturers such as de Havilland had turned their sights to more lucrative military contracts as well as prestigious and expensive civilian projects. Military surplus (cheap) Tiger Moths, Austers and later the advanced Chipmunks satisfied some demand but the more modern types, faster, comfortable and affordable, came flooding in from the USA.

The first of the many Cessna types was a Cessna 175A (four-seater) that arrived crated at Panshanger in March 1960 and was test-flown on 18 March by chief pilot Joe Tyszcko. The smaller Cessna 150, in the form of G-APXY, arrived at Panshanger after July that year. An aircraft sales centre was established inside the hangar designed to show off all of the Cessna types using a car-showroom style approach.

Above left: The 'T2' hangar was constructed during the latter part of 1959 as part of the aerodrome expansion. The hangar was built from new parts and not taken from a disused airfield since it has peculiar internal dimensions. Airwork Services used the hangar to complete Cessna kits and sell finished aircraft via a 'car-showroom' sales and service centre. Later the hangar was used for private aircraft and Autair Helicopter Services. This view, from 1984, shows it rather sad and neglected. (Author)

Above right: The Cessna 150 was the first of many modern, all-metal Cessna light aircraft imported into the UK and was a major contributor to the demise of the British light aeroplane. The completion of the large T2 hangar at Panshanger in 1960 for Airwork Services allowed kits to be imported, assembled and sold via a sales, marketing and servicing franchise. Completed Cessna aircraft were test-flown from Panshanger until Airwork moved away in 1963. G-APXY was a 1958-model Cessna 150 (17711) registered in January 1960 to Shackleton Aviation and Airwork Services from July 1960. It was kept at Panshanger until sold to D. Westoby at Squires Gate on 17 April 1961. (MAP)

Airwork Services registered Cessna 175A G-ARCK in kit form in November 1960 and it was based until sold to the Wells Organisation (Wellsair) in October 1961. (NA3T/ATPH Transportphotos)

W.S. Shackleton Aviation began an aircraft sales centre in the T2 hangar during 1960, though this seems to have been a temporary affair, the company later consolidating itself at Baginton, Coventry. Airwork Services remained at Panshanger until June 1963, though the last aircraft was registered in November 1961 after which they imported Cessna aircraft through Hurn (Bournemouth) instead. The T2 hangar remained in use for the Lotus Car Co., the storage of based aircraft and, later, Autair Helicopters. At least one television advertisement used the hangar as a location (Milk Marketing Board) with a huge facsimile of a milk bottle dominating the scene for a few months in the lean years of the mid-1970s.

Top: Registered when new in May 1960 to Vigors Aviation, Oxford, the Piper agents, Piper PA-18 Super Cub 95, G-ARAO, was sold to Rent-a-Plane in July 1960 and leased to the London Aeroplane Club for about two years until it was sold to N.H. Pennington in October 1962. (Graham Lewis)

Middle: The PA-22 Tri-Pacer was Piper's attempt to compete with the Cessna range of light touring aircraft emerging in the 1950s and filled a gap between the steel and fabric 'tail-dragger' Super Cub and the all-metal Cherokee. G-ARAE had been previously registered in Holland as PH-RAC and moved to the UK for E. Wein in May 1960. By August 1960 it moved to L.R. Davies and is seen here at Panshanger. It was damaged on 16 April 1962 and rebuilt later by Thurston Engineering at Stapleford. (NA3T/ATPH Transportphotos)

Bottom: The Cessna 182C model marked the introduction of the swept fin and rudder to the 210hp, four-seat tourer. Registered in April 1960 to H. Detering and Airwork Services from August 1960, G-ARAA had a very short life. On 6 May 1961 it crashed into St Catherines Hill, Blackgang, Isle of Wight, with fatal results. Parts of the wreckage were returned to Panshanger in June. (NA3T/ATPH Transportphotos)

Imported by Rent-a-Plane in October 1960 and leased to the London Aeroplane Club during 1963, Piper PA-18 Super Cub 95 G-ARCT was used only briefly until it was sold to J. Braithwaite (Aerial Photos) by April 1963. (Dave Bray)

By February 1961 the Airwork assembly line at Panshanger was in full flow and Cessna 175B, G-ARFM, one of a batch of seven registered. It was sold to P.W. Ingram in April 1961 at Panshanger and by December 1962 had moved to Eastleigh. (NA3T/ATPH Transportphotos)

Opposite above: Another Piper PA-18 Super Cub 95 leased from Rent-a-Plane by the London Aeroplane Club was G-ARBX, used from January 1961 until mid-1963. (NA3T/ATPH Transportphotos)

Opposite middle: The Piper PA-22 Caribbean 150 was a low-cost version of the Tri Pacer and G-ARCB had been imported via Vigors Aviation in June 1960 and leased to the London Aeroplane Club from August that year. It was sold to D.J. Porter of Flair Avia Ltd at Biggin Hill in December 1962. (NA3T/ATPH Transportphotos)

Opposite below: In October 1960 Airwork received the attractive Cessna 310 for resale. The 310D model sported the swept fin and rudder. G-ARCH moved north to Perth for Airwork Service Training the following year. (NA3T/ATPH Transportphotos)

The interior of the T2 taken in August 1961 shows the car-showroom style used by Airwork for marketing and sales of the Cessna products. In view is Cessna 175B, G-ARMM; Cessna 172, G-ARMO; Cessna 310D, G-ARCI; Cessna 180A, G-ARLC (owned by Colin Chapman) and Cessna 185, G-ARMJ – the subject of an *Aeroplane Magazine* flight test. (*AEROPLANE MONTHLY*/www.aeroplanemonthly.com)

Registered to Airwork Services at Panshanger in July 1961, Cessna 175B Skylark G-ARMM was sold by March 1964 to R.R. Kearsley and noted at Sywell by January 1965. (NA3T/ATPH Transportphotos)

Cessna 185 Skywagon G-ARMJ sits on the grass outside the T2 hangar in August 1961. Formerly N9900X and registered on 12 July 1961 to Airwork Services Panshanger, the Cessna 185 was used for demonstrations by Airwork until sold to Shackleton Aviation in August 1963. (*AEROPLANE MONTHLY*/www.aeroplanemonthly.com)

The Piper PA-22 Colt 108 was a lower-powered version of the Tri Pacer and G-ARKT arrived at Panshanger on lease from Rent-a-Plane in March 1962. By May 1963 it had moved to Barton for Light Planes (Lancashire Ltd). (Grant Peerless)

LONDON TO CARDIFF AIR RACE

The 2 June 1961 marked the start of the London to Cardiff Air Race as a precursor for the Cardiff Air Display the following day. Entrants had arrived at Panshanger for refuelling a few days earlier and at least two Spitfires graced the turf. One Belgian-registered Spitfire IX, OO-ARE (Race number 100), arrived from Southend on 27 May and departed for Cardiff on 2 June but after the air-speed indicator failed in-flight the pilot, Beverley Snook, made an emergency landing at Exeter; after turning off the engine the port wing exploded due to a fuel malfunction. At least thirty-five aircraft made the journey safely (see Appendix 6).

This aerial shot was taken on 2 June 1961, the morning of the London to Cardiff Air Race, eventually won by Viv Bellamy flying the two-seat Spitfire, G-AIDN. This can be seen next to the fuel pumps. The ill-fated Spitfire IX, OO-ARE, is parked by the eastern edge of the long brick hangar. Thirty-five aircraft reached Cardiff. Keegan Aviation aircraft can be seen on the north side of the runway and a lone de Havilland Dragon Rapide sits by the large blister hangar. (Airviews/ Simmons Aerofilms)

The Luton Minor was a successful ultra-light, high wing monoplane designed by C.H. Latimer-Needham and built by Luton Aircraft Ltd at Barton-in-the-Clay, Bedfordshire. After modifications and a factory move to the Phoenix Works at Gerrards Cross in Buckinghamshire, the company offered the aircraft for home construction. G-AFIR was the first of these and built by J.S. Squires at Rearsby from 1937–1938 and registered on 7 July 1938, powered by a 35hp Anzani engine. It survived the war and was completely rebuilt at Pinner by Arthur W.J.G. Ord-Hume and fitted first with a 38hp Menguin and later a 40hp JAP engine. It is shown here at Panshanger in 1961. (NA3T/ATPH Transportphotos)

A rare visitor to Panshanger for the 1961 London to Cardiff Air Race was Vickers Supermarine Spitfire Tr.8, G-AIDN. Owned at the time by Viv Bellamy at Eastleigh, the Spitfire arrived at Panshanger on 1 June 1961 and became the eventual winner of the race the following day, which marked the precursor for the Cardiff Air Display. 'IDN was registered on 7 January 1947 and sold by Bellamy to John Fairey in August 1963. It is currently based in the USA. (Richard Riding)

Another race entrant was Comper Swift, G–ABUS, registered to A.J. Linnell of Sywell. (Richard Riding)

Another Spitfire, this time a Spitfire LF.IXe, registered to Beverley Snook of Trans Global Aviation Supply. The Spitfire was built at Castle Bromwich for the RAF as NH238, joining 84 Group Support Unit. It passed to the Royal Netherlands Air Force on 30 May 1947 and served in Java before being sold to the Belgian Air Force in 1950. It was used by a civil target tug company, COGEA Nouvelles, based on Ostende and registered OO-ARE from 8 September 1956 until May 1961, when purchased by Snook and delivered to Panshanger on 27 May. It was flown by Beverley Snook in the London to Cardiff Air Race on 2 June but the ASI failed causing a precautionary landing at Exeter. During shut down of the engine the port wing exploded due to a vapour lock and the Spitfire was badly damaged. After repairs it was sold in the USA and returned to the UK in 1983, being registered G-MKIX. (Richard Riding)

LOTUS CARS

In October 1959 Lotus Cars moved to Delamere Road, Cheshunt, after outgrowing premises in Hornsey Lane. Very soon the company outgrew these buildings and founder and chairman Colin Chapman moved the Service Department of the company to Panshanger where he had started a small flying club. Lotus Cars used a Miles Messenger (G-AKIO) from 1961 and as the company flourished, more modern types, including the Piper Comanche (G-ARIN from 1962 and G-ARYV from 1963). Chapman was an avid pilot and founded the connection of the motor racing fraternity with aviation by flying to racing events. After the introduction of the Lotus Elite kit car owner-constructors were encouraged to drive their cars to the aerodrome and have them checked by the Works Department. The Lotus group moved to Hethel in Norfolk by the mid-1960s.

After a period registered in Holland, Miles M.38 Messenger 2A, G-AKIO was restored to owners A.G. Wilson Ltd in August 1960. Owner of Lotus Cars, Colin Chapman, was looking for a suitable company aircraft to pursue his interest in aviation and commute to racing events. 'KIO was purchased in October 1960 and based at Panshanger at the time the company was developing the Lotus Elite kit car and used the aerodrome as an engineering centre to check kit-built cars. Seen here at Panshanger on 28 April 1963 'KIO was soon replaced with Lotus Cars by a modern Piper Comanche and sold to A. Rayner of Brentwood by February 1964. (Graham Lewis)

This Piper PA-24 Comanche 250, G-ARYV, was registered on 17 April 1962 to Colin Chapman of Lotus Cars at Panshanger, replacing G-ARIN. It had carried the US registration N7337P previously. The photograph was taken on 28 April 1963 and Lotus Cars moved away from Panshanger later in the year. (Graham Lewis)

DAVID CARNEGIE

Local businessman David Carnegie, director of Carnegie Chemicals in Welwyn Garden City, learned to fly with the LAC in 1951 and purchased a Miles Messenger (G-AGPX) for the purposes of his tuition and his four sons. In turn CFI Dennis Cather tutored the family. On 30 May 1962 David Carnegie had a narrow escape in his new Mooney M.21, G-APVV, which suffered engine failure after take-off and force-landed in a nearby field. CFI Tommy Thompson and assistant Pat Doyle were amazed to find Mr Carnegie unhurt and fortunately damage to the aircraft was slight. The Carnegie Flying Group was based on the aerodrome during 1963.

PARIS FLYING GROUP

The Paris Flying Group lost its only Tiger Moth, G-AOFD, on 16 September 1962 when pilot Ian Curr of Boreham Wood crash-landed near South Lodge cottages in Herns Lane after the engine failed on take-off. Arthur Berry, Mr Curr's passenger, was hurt.

Powered by two 130hp Gipsy Major engines, the ST-12 Monospar was built by General Aircraft Ltd at Hanworth, Feltham in 1935 and as its name suggests was a monoplane fitted with a cantilever wing. VH-UTH was the first exported example and one of two delivered to New England Airways in Australia. It survived service and on 22 August 1961 was flown back to the UK by Dr John Morris and Bruce Harrison, arriving at Lympne on 30 November. By December 1961 it arrived at Panshanger for storage when the wings were removed. It was believed to have moved to Croydon by 1965. The Monospar was passed to the Newark Air Museum in 1968. (Maurice Freeman)

This Tiger Moth served the war as DF194 though most of the time it was in storage. Sold in November 1953 to Continental Aircraft Services (of the Panshanger Proctor fame) it was not civilianised until February 1959, being registered G–AOFD and purchased by J.R. Burnett. In April 1961 'OFD was purchased by W.W. Goodman, operating from Panshanger as the Paris Flying Group. On 16 September 1962 pilot Ian Curr and passenger Arthur Berry took off from the aerodrome into a gusty head wind. The Tiger virtually stalled in the climb and the pilot, unable to recover the aircraft, force-landed near Stone Lodge cottages, Herns Lane. The aircraft hit a tree and was wrecked, with injuries occurring to Mr Berry. (*Welwyn Hatfield Times*/WGC Library)

Registered new in January 1956 to Hunting Clan Transport at Luton Auster, J-5P Autocar, G-AOGM, came to Panshanger in June 1957 with new owner J.D. Coleman. It was based until February 1964 after which it moved to Elstree for a new life as a survey aircraft for Hunting's. Noted at Panshanger in the late 1950s with a long-range fuel tank under the fuselage. (Dave Bray)

KEEGAN AVIATION

In the early 1960s Mr Thomas 'Mike' D. Keegan, later of BKS Air Transport (the 'K'), Transglobe and Transmeridian Airways, began several aviation enterprises, some based at Panshanger. One of the earliest was Kay Rings Ltd, which dealt with the sale of new and used aircraft as well as their lease to other companies. Kay Rings was headquartered at Panshanger from January 1960 until the end of 1961 when the company folded. Associated companies included Airline Air Spares, Bembridge Air Hire (also known as Bembridge Car Hire), Keegan Aviation, Keystone (Southend) Finance Co. and Trans World Leasing.

Keegan Aviation imported Aero Commander and Cessna 310 executive twins into Panshanger for resale and were the UK agents for Riley Aircraft (Riley 65 = Cessna 310).

The same company used de Havilland Doves for communications and liaison between Keegan's various operations, basing them at Panshanger. Keegan used the former Agricultural Aviation Co. 69' Miskin blister hangar on the north site for many aircraft being traded or used for communications. During 1963 Keegan bought and leased the Scottish Aviation Twin Pioneer of which three ex-Iran examples were placed at Panshanger. The group traded in larger types, too, and noted gracing the turf from 1961 until 1963 was a Vickers Viking, G-AHPB, from the defunct Overseas Aviation, a Douglas C-54 (G-ARIC) and two Canadair C-4 Argonauts (DC-4 with Rolls-Royce Merlin engines), purchased from the same concern. The Viking went on to fly with Autair International at Luton in 1963, whilst the C-54 and an Argonaut (CF-TFE) were sold on. CF-TFN, the other Argonaut, still in Trans Canada Airlines colours but stripped of many internal parts, languished until it was broken up at Luton in 1964.

In December 1962 an item in Air Pictorial noted, 'A new British independent, Transmeridian Flying Services Ltd, is to start charter flights with one DC-4 (G-APID sub leased from Kay Rings) based at Panshanger'. No evidence for this operation starting can be found.

Keegan outgrew Panshanger and relocated to Southend and Stansted by the mid-1960s. Trans World Leasing of Panshanger (another Keegan Co.) traded in the 'heavier' types, namely Bristol Freighter, Vickers Viking and Douglas DC-4/C-54. Most found new homes readily and were unlikely to have been stored at the aerodrome for long.

Opposite top: An early example of the successful de Havilland DH.104 Dove, this Mk.1 (04024) was delivered new to South Africa, becoming ZS-AVH in May 1947 with Consolidated Investments Anglo Transvaal. It returned to the UK and became G-AMRN in April 1952 for Stewart Smith & Co. Ltd and modified to become a Dove 2 around this time, moving to Bristol Aircraft in July 1956. Sold to T.D. Keegan Ltd in August 1957 as a Dove 6, the photograph shows it at Panshanger in late 1961 being used as a crew transport for Keegan Aviation's leasing and ferrying businesses. G-AMRN was sold in January 1963 to Bentley (Plant Hire) Ltd. (NA3T/ATPH Transportphotos)

Opposite middle: The Dove 2B was an executive variant of the Mk.1 powered by two 340hp Gipsy Queen 70-4 engines and this aircraft was sold in July 1948 to the Maharajah Karni Singhi of Bikaner and registered in India as VT-CVA. It returned to the UK as G-ANGE on 12 November 1953 with BKS Air Transport (Engineering). The initials 'BKS' were the first letters of the surnames Barnby, Keegan & Stevens and the aircraft became closely associated with Keegan Aviation as a result. BKS Engineering maintained the airline fleet and operated communication flights. Later the engineering team operated aerial survey flights. In September 1960 G-ANGE was leased to Tyne Tees Air Charter, a Newcastle-based airline helped greatly by Mike Keegan. By December 1961 Keegan Aviation took over the aircraft for leasing and by February 1962 it had moved to Libyan Aviation sub-leased to Metropolitan Air Movements. It was damaged beyond repair in a forced landing in Libya on 26 February 1964. (NA3T/ATPH Transportphotos)

Above: The Percival P.40 Prentice was designed to meet a post-war requirement of a basic trainer for the RAF but suffered many changes to the original specification and as a result proved generally disappointing in service. Large numbers came available in the mid-1950s with 252 being purchased by Aviation Traders Ltd for conversion to civilian use. In the event most were scrapped at Southend, Stansted and Minxworth but a few survived including 'OMK, despite a strange history. In RAF service with 22FTS as VS374, the Prentice was sold on 25 April 1956, becoming G-AOLR initially, but swapping identities with the original G-AOMK (VR304) which in turn had been registered on 22 May 1956. The new 'OLR crashed at Kilsythe on 30 July 1961 and 'OMK was purchased by T.D. (Mike) Keegan in July 1959 and is seen at Panshanger in 1961. It was sold to Steels Aviation at Lulsgate in April 1962. (NA3T/ATPH Transportphotos)

Keegan Aviation was appointed agents for the Aero Commander executive twin and Aero Commander 520, G-ARJJ, registered to them in May 1961. This early example is seen at Panshanger in 1962 before sale to R.M. Wilson in August that year. After several owners it was destroyed by fire at Fairoaks on 19 August 1969. (NA3T/ATPH Transportphotos)

The Riley 65 was a 'cleaned up' variant of the successful Cessna 310 executive twin and in 1961 Keegan Aviation was appointed sole European distributors for the type. G-ARRR was registered to Keegan Aviation at Panshanger on 16 August 1961 but sold to Switzerland under a month later, becoming HB-LBN. It is seen here during this brief period near the large Miskin blister on the north site. Keegan's Aero Commander aircraft, G-ARJJ, is behind it. (NA3T/ATPH Transportphotos)

The utilitarian Scottish Aviation Twin Pioneer was a rugged, light transport, powered by Alvis Leonides radial engines. Keegan Aviation imported two in March 1963 for resale and G-ASJS was parked for a few months next to the Canadair C-4, CF-TFN. It was sold in Norway during August 1963, becoming LN-BFK. (Maurice Freeman)

Opposite above: A strange visitor to Panshanger in 1962 was a Swiss-registered Pilatus PC-6 Porter, HB-FAM. The Porter was a utility aircraft powered by a 350hp Lycoming engine. This Porter first flew in April 1962 and was used by the Pilatus Co. until 29 August 1963, being modified by A.D.S. (Aerial) Ltd at Southend as a crop sprayer and used for trials in Sudan. It was transferred to the British register as G-ASTO on 3 June 1964 for A.D.S. and used until August 1965 in Sudan. Sold to Keegan Aviation in October 1965 it was converted to a Mk.2 and sold in Algeria on 9 February 1967 becoming 7T-VBV. (NA3T/ATPH Transportphotos)

Opposite middle: G-ARIC, a Douglas C-54A-DC Skymaster, is pictured here on 7 January 1962 in World Wide Aviation titles. It was registered to T.D. Keegan on 1 December 1960, to subsidiary Trans World Leasing in January 1961 and to Capt. W.J. Bright's World Wide Aviation in July 1961. It remained with World Wide carrying out charter flights until returned to Keegan at Panshanger in November 1961. It was resident until April 1962 when it was sold in the Belgian Congo as 9Q-RIC. World Wide finally ceased operations in July 1962 and Bill Bright was taken on by the Keegan group. (Graham Lewis)

Above: Vickers Viking 1A G–AHPB (132) was registered to Hunting Air Travel in 1950 and stayed with the Hunting Group until sold to Overseas Aviation (CI) Ltd in 1961. It is pictured here in these titles on 7 January 1962, having arrived at Panshanger on 14 December 1961 by Transworld Leasing, a Keegan company. It departed to Autair at Luton in April 1963 and is now preserved as D–BABY at the Technorama Museum, Winterthur, Switzerland. (Graham Lewis)

This Canadair C-4M2 North Star CF-TFE arrived in December 1961 for one of T.D. Keegan's enterprises but departed to Baginton, Coventry, shortly afterwards on 14 January 1962. It was photographed on 7 January 1962 in Overseas Aviation

The North Star was Trans Canada Airlines' version of the Canadian derivative of the Douglas DC-4 airliner; the main difference involved the use of Rolls-Royce Merlin 500 engines in place of American radials. BOAC used a variant named the Argonaut during the 1950s. In 1960 charter company Overseas Aviation purchased a number of Trans Canada machines for inclusive tour flights to Europe in the summer season. The company floundered and their aircraft were purchased by Keegan Aviation through A.J. Gaul. Two arrived at Panshanger late in 1961. Shown here in early 1962 is CF-TFN languishing next to the T2 hangar until flown to Luton and onwards for scrapping. The remarkable thing about the aircraft was the sheer size compared to other types using the airfield and just how marginal the runway length must have been for take off.

Keegan Aviation kept spares for the North Stars in the large Miskin blister on the north site, where complete Merlin 'power eggs' could be seen. For many years afterwards Trans Canada Airlines paraphernalia could be found in the woods and huts nearby. (David Bray)

EVENTS

Easter 1962 saw a Tiger Club display at Panshanger, the first of several. These displays were exciting local events attempting to portray the thrilling 'barnstorming' air displays of the 1930s. The Tiger Club fielded air racing with French-designed Druine Turbulents, aerobatics from Tiger Moth and Arrow Active and such novelty acts as a windswept soul strapped to the top of a Tiger Moth wing. These Easter displays were repeated through the early 1960s.

Occasional summer displays were held during the 1960s, including a Tiger Club display on 15 April 1963.

Registered to the London Aeroplane Club in May 1963, Piper PA-23 Aztec 250 G-ARXF replaced the earlier Piper Apache (G-APCL). It remained on strength until sold to T.M. Snart at Leicester East by 1968. It is seen here at Panshanger in 1963. (NA3T/ATPH Transportphotos)

Aerial Farm Services acquired this Boeing A75-N1 Stearman, G-AROY, in June 1961 and, powered by a 450hp Pratt & Whitney radial, this extra performance provided additional safety in its role as a crop sprayer. W.A. Jordan of Jordans Foods used the aircraft for many years and it was a regular visitor to Panshanger. Spectacular take offs using the available concrete hardstanding was a speciality. Photograph taken in 1978. (David Oliver)

Left: Welwyn & Hatfield Times advertisement for the Tiger Club Air Display on 15 April 1963. (*Welwyn Hatfield Times*)

Below: In late summer 1962 four Piper PA-18 Super Cubs arrived at Panshanger in kit form from Heathrow and were assembled on site. They were registered to Aerospray Cyprus and after air tests flown to Southend during September 1962 for crating and delivery to Nicosia. 5B-CAC is seen here with others in the Keegan hangar on the north side of the airfield. The wings of the first production de Havilland Dove lie against the rear wall of the hangar. (NA3T/ATPH Transportphotos)

PIPER SUPER CUBS

In the late summer of 1962 four new Piper Super Cubs arrived, in parts, from Heathrow and were erected on site. They were registered to Aerospray in Cyprus and delivered there via Southend on 9 September to become some of the first aircraft on the new register.

THE FRENCH INVASION

During 1962 the club re-equipped with the French-built Morane Saulnier Rallye with eight aircraft imported for resale and five retained during 1963. During the early 1960s the club leased a few Piper Super Cubs and Caribbean (a deluxe Tri-Pacer) aircraft.

By 1963 the London Aeroplane Club (also abbreviated to London Aero Club by this time) remained the aerodrome owners (J N Somers AFC) with Phyllis Somers as club secretary and P.T. Andrews as the aerodrome manager. The club could be contacted on Essendon 305. Two Piper Super Cubs, a Chipmunk and the twin-engine Piper Apache (G-APCL) completed the club inventory and membership topped 150.

The French-built Morane Saulnier MS.880B Rallye Club was a very successful club
and touring aircraft designed in the late 1950s. London Aeroplane Club became the
agents for sale and distribution of the type in 1961 and G-ARTT, the eighth built,
was the first example of the type on the UK register, arriving in December that year.
'RTT was sold to J.N. Appleyard in March 1963 and subsequently had many owners.
Currently it is stored in Knutsford. (NA3T/ATPH Transportphotos)

In May 1962 the London Aeroplane Club imported Morane Saulnier MS.885
Super Rallye, G-ASAO. It was sold in June 1964 to J. Sandys. (NA3T/ATPH
Transportphotos)

WELWYN, PANDAS AND KINGFISHERS

Panshanger was also home to the Welwyn Flying Group, secretary John Hercus, using a Piper
Tri-Pacer, G-ARDT and the Biggleswade Flying Group with a Tiger Moth G-ANSP. The
Panda Flying Club had operated a Miles Hawk Major, G-ADWT, between 1958 and 1961,
moving to Germany and back to Luton by April 1963. Their CFI was Derek de Sarigny, who
later became closely affiliated with the aerodrome.

The Kingfisher Flying Group was based at the aerodrome during the early 1960s, operating
a single Auster 4; the club chairman was Harry Judd.

In July 1965 Pan Aeronautics was set up by Nat Somers to operate as a flying centre
replacing the London Aeroplane Club. The club operated a two-seat Ercoupe 415D from
4 July (G-ATFP). On 2 April 1966 the Ercoupe made a forced landing 4 miles south of the
aerodrome after the pilot, Mr Benson, ran into bad weather.

By this time Nat Somers was heavily involved in other activities, notably managing
Southampton Airport and as a result the London Aeroplane Club ceased to operate its own
aircraft. However, there were other plans for the aerodrome (see next section).

Pan Aeronautics organised an official opening fly-in and open day on 15 August 1965. On
4 September 1966 the club organised an air display to commemorate the fiftieth anniversary
of the shooting down of the German airship near Cuffley.

The Wasp Flying Group began operations at Panshanger in the early 1960s using several Auster J-1's and Miles Messengers, the CFI being Derek de Sarigny in the early years. The group continued in active flying training until the rise of the Panshanger School of Flying in the early 1980s.

On 22 January 1967 an Auster J-1 registered to the London Aeroplane Club/Wasp Flying Group, G-AGVL, crashed near Panshanger after the engine failed. The pilot, Mr Wallace Lipka, suffered a broken leg and the passengers, Adele Snewing and Chris Foreman, were slightly injured.

It is 15 May 1965 and the annual Tiger Club Air Display. Tiger Moth G-ACDC and G-ANMZ have standing-on-the-wing modifications. G-ANMZ (left) was heavily modified with a 145hp Gipsy Major engine and fuel tank moved to the front cockpit to provide higher speed, better aerodynamics and aerobatic performance. 'NMZ crashed at Challock on 22 May 1969 and was not repaired.
G-ACDC remains the oldest airworthy Tiger Moth though had several complete rebuilds during her life. (Maurice Freeman)

G-APAL gets airborne from Panshanger in 1966. (Gerry Cullen)

Tiger Moth G-ANSP had served the war as DE877 until sold for civilian use in June 1954 to the Luton Flying Club. It came to Panshanger in January 1955 registered to the Biggleswade Flying Group and was used until severely damaged on take off from Panshanger on 1 July 1968, which was a little over a month after the author's first flight in the aircraft. The wreck was taken to Booker by October 1968 and rebuilt to fly in the hands of Personal Plane Services. It was shown at Hatfield during the 1969 Open Day and sold in South Africa in February 1970, becoming ZS-JVZ.

The photograph shows a view of the white Laing hut used by the London Aeroplane Club during the late 1950s and early 1960s. To the right is the much modified blister hangar erected at the same time over the old coal storage area. (Gerry Cullen)

Registered in the USA as N99545, the Ercoupe 415D/CD was built by the Engineering & Research Corporation at Riversdale and incorporated a strange, linked rudder and aileron control. The 415D was powered by an 85hp Continental engine. G-ATFP was imported and registered on 28 June 1965 to Panaeronautics, a club born from the ashes of the London Aeroplane Club, with Derek de Sarigny as the CFI. 'TFP was not a success (nor was the club) and sold on quickly to K.F.P. Couling by March 1967. The photograph was taken on 15 August 1965. (Graham Lewis)

Registered on 24 July 1963, Piper PA-28 Cherokee 180B G-ASKT was based at Panshanger from early 1964 with Madison Artists until sold to R.J. Cysters & Partners in October 1969. (Gerry Cullen)

Registered on 10 January 1963 to CSE Aviation, the importers of Piper aircraft, Piper PA-28 Cherokee 180B, G-ASEJ, was a typical example of the modern all-metal touring aircraft coming from the USA. It is noted at Panshanger during 1966 when owned by J. Wilding. It remained until sold in June 1972 to J.J. Smith. (Gerry Cullen)

Above left: The Thruxton Jackaroo was a four-seat cabin adaptation of the de Havilland Tiger Moth. Eighteen were built by Jackaroo Aircraft at Thruxton from 1957 until 1959, with another constructed by Rollason. G-APAL had served the war as N6849 (as a Tiger Moth) until pensioned off and registered for civilian use on 4 April 1957. It arrived at Panshanger with the Stevenage Flying Group in June 1965 (registered to Maurice Brett on 11 October 1965) and is seen here during the 1966 air display. By February 1968 'PAL had moved to Bedfordshire. (Gerry Cullen)

Above right: Registered on 11 February 1946 to Rollason Aircraft and Engines at Croydon, Auster J-1 Autocrat G-AHAU was one of a number from a cancelled Swiss order. After a few owners it arrived at Panshanger in February 1967, registered to Derek C.B. de Sarigny, CFI of the Wasp Flying Group, and was photographed around this time. By May 1976 Brian Foley became the new owner, moving to Little Gransden later. 'HAU was later sold on, fitted with a 160hp Lycoming engine and re-engineered with a modified fin, similar to the Beagle Husky. (MAP)

Opposite below: One of many Auster aircraft based at Panshanger over the years, J-1 Autocrat G-AGVL (1871) was operated by the London Aeroplane Club from April 1964 and within a year moved to R.D. Stirk of the Wasp Flying Group. On 22 January 1967 Wallace Lipka was taking off from the airfield with two passengers when the engine lost power. At a height of 150ft the aircraft stalled during a rapid return back to the airfield and the port wing hit the ground causing the 'GVL to dig in and nose over. The pilot suffered a broken leg and the passengers, Adele Snewing and Chris Foreman, had minor injuries. (*Welwyn Hatfield Times*/WGC Library)

Above left: This Auster J-1 Autocrat (2159) arrived at Panshanger in 1965, registered to R.D. Stirk of the Wasp Flying Group. In May 1965 it was registered to Derek de Sarigny of the same group and remained at Panshanger through the 1970s, departing for Little Gransden under Brian Beeston's charge. (Author)

Above right: Masquerading as a Luftwaffe aircraft for the 1958 film *Operation Bullshine*, this Airspeed Oxford 2, G-AHGU, is seen next to the boiler house and dope store on the south site. Filming took place for six months over the winter of 1958–59 when the aircraft departed. It was sold to John Crewdson of Overseas Aviation in July 1960. Significantly the roof trusses of the brickwalled hangar can be seen under construction to the rear. (NA3T/ATPH Transportphotos)

CONTINUED COUNCIL CONFLICT

The on-going battles with the council continued during the 1960s as there were concerns about the club's interpretation of restriction orders on aerodrome operations. During a meeting with the council in February 1964, the London Aeroplane Club insisted the aerodrome should expand and operate services to provide a sound financial future. The council provided future plans for Panshanger housing and used examples of recent accidents at the aerodrome to highlight the dangers for the future. The council even proposed an alternative aerodrome situated on the council waste tip at Cole Green, to the south-east side of the town, roughly bordered by the A414. This would have involved the closure and removal of the WGC-Hertford railway.

The London Aeroplane Club had proposed that lock-up hangars be constructed but this was not allowed because the council noted that some of the existing hangars were not being used for aircraft.

New approach and take-off procedures were planned for the future as the council had by now purchased all land up to the southern and western boundaries and by 1965 had begun to construct the first phase of Panshanger housing.

Registered out of sequence in February 1959 to suit its owner, Air
Commodore G.J.C. Paul, the diminutive Druine D.31 Turbulent was a
successful French design for homebuilders. G-AJCP arrived at Panshanger in
June 1966 registered to N.H. Kempt and painted in a pale green scheme. It
was based there until sold to H.J. Shaw in September 1978. The photograph
was taken in 1976 showing repairs to the blister hangar on the south site,
which had been built in the 1950s on the old coal storage area from salvaged
parts from the north site. The donor skeletal hangar remains. (MAP)

The Wasp Flying Group used J-1 Autocrat G-AJEI from spring 1968 until the
mid-1970s. In this poor box Brownie shot from April 1968 the maintenance
hangar also contains Auster G-AGVN and Messenger G-AJYZ and the CFI,
Derek de Sarigny. The Messenger survived until mid-June 1968 when it was
damaged in a landing accident at Panshanger and considered too costly to
repair. It languished on the north site being broken up by vandals and the
elements until burned by 1970. (Author)

In October 1965 the council received details from Nat Somer's architects proposing a
comprehensive development of the aerodrome into a housing estate. The council rejected
the plan as their housing needs for the future were already catered for. Clear now was the
change in tactics adopted by the aerodrome owner upon understanding the aerodrome could
not expand due to encroachment of housing and the subsequent need to seek a way out.
In October 1967 Nat Somers tried again and proposed the site be developed as a wholesale
warehouse, for light industrial use or as offices. Again this was refused, due to the council's
green belt policy.

FIRST FLIGHTS

Panshanger was chosen for a number of first flights during the 1960s. During 1962 a Bensen B-7M autogyro G-ARFE was test flown, being registered to S. Rymill of Brookmans Park. No certificate of airworthiness was issued for this machine.

The unique Gowland GWG.2 Jenny Wren (G-ASRF) was test-flown from Panshanger on 13 October 1966.

In 1968 the Andreasson BA-4B biplane sports aircraft prototype SE-XBS arrived at Panshanger and was air-tested by Peter Philips prior to becoming G-AWPZ. From Rush Green came the diminutive Owl Racer, G-AYMS, based there over Easter 1971. It was air-tested from Panshanger shortly afterwards but sadly crashed at Greenwich on 31 May 1971 after losing its propeller, killing legendary pilot 'Manx' Kelly. On 10 September 1973 J.R. Coates' pretty Swalesong SA.11 home-built design, G-AYDV, made its first flight from the aerodrome.

The Gowland GWG.2 Jenny Wren was a much-modified Luton Minor homebuilt designed by Jack Gowland and built at his Brookmans Park home, utilizing the wings of Minor, G-AGEP. The large, fully-enclosed cockpit held pilot and a child in tandem. Final assembly took place at Panshanger during 1966. Its permit to fly expired on 4 June 1971 and the aircraft stored at Brookmans Park. It is currently at Flixton, Norfolk. (MAP)

Serving in the RAF as WB734 until sold from storage at Aston Down, DHC-1 Chipmunk 22 G-AOZP was registered on 14 February 1957. It is noted at Panshanger in late 1969 registered to M.E. Darlington. 'OZP is currently based in Doncaster (2004). (MAP)

Into the 1970s

PANSHANGER FLYING SCHOOL

A reassuring plan for the aerodrome to be developed as a commercial concern with the formation of the Panshanger Flying School in July 1969 attracted interest in the local newspapers. Mrs R.L. de Sarigny, the secretary, stated that the current owners of aircraft housed on the aerodrome would not be affected by the formation of the new club. Three Cessna 150 aircraft arrived from Leavesden to form the club aircraft nucleus and a single Rollason Condor provided 'tail wheel' experience. The CFI was Derek de Sarigny and the school could be contacted on Essendon 534, offering a trial lesson for £3.5.0 (£3.25). The school was active for two years or so until closed over Christmas 1970.

Panshanger held its last official public air display on 2 August 1970 with a varied selection of visiting aircraft including the Army 'Blue Eagles' helicopter display and the 'Rothmans' Stampe aerobatic teams.

The informality of these events is now lost forever following restrictions placed on air display operations. It is recalled that during the display a very well-known pilot and MP took-off in his vintage Morane Saulnier MS.230 to give an elegant and tight aerobatic performance over the council waste tip at Cole Green. This was quietly explained upon his arrival back at Panshanger where the crowd had been staring into space for fifteen minutes.

During March 1971 Bert and Doreen Benson of Welwyn Garden City formed the Hertford Flying Club to take over flying training. Barely six weeks later, the club folded, the founders claiming 'impossible conditions' imposed by the aerodrome owners. This seemed to be a common view of aerodrome operations at the time, with much being made of plans by the aerodrome owners in the local press to sell the aerodrome land for building. Costs for hangarage and facilities rose steeply at Panshanger and clubs could not function. The aerodrome lost its operating license later in 1971.

An aerial photograph of the aerodrome taken in May 1972 records the buildings to be relatively intact though the control tower was not operational at this time. It was quite usual to visit the north site and discover large quantities of RAF surplus uniforms and survival kits. The hangars here often revealed a treasure trove of aircraft parts, mainly spare Proctor and Anson windscreens, and some larger components too.

THE BARNSTORMERS PRESENT
AT PANSHANGER AERODROME
Nr. Welwyn Garden City
on Sun. Aug. 2nd.

air display

SW30

Right: Welwyn Times & Hatfield Herald
advertisement for the Barnstormers Air Display
on 2 August 1970. (*Welwyn Hatfield Times*)

Above left: Registered on 30 August 1946 to G.H.B. Linnell at Wellingborough, Messenger 2A,
G-AIDK, was a hybrid, retaining the square side windows of the military Mk.1 but built with a 155hp
Blackburn Cirrus Major engine. 'IDK moved to Elstree in March 1967, owned by D.C. Johnson, and
was at Panshanger by July 1968. It was sold to Derek de Sarigny of the Wasp Flying Group by
31 July 1968 and used until sold on to Messrs J.M. Lovett and S.W. Ward at Panshanger. It is seen here
on 2 August 1970 during the Panshanger Air Display. It was sold on 29 January 1974 and moved to
Bedfordshire. (Graham Lewis)

Above right: Rollason Aircraft and Engines constructed a club version of the French homebuilt
design, the Druine Condor. G-AWSN was fitted with a 100hp Rolls-Royce Continental engine and
registered to N.H. Jones of the Tiger Club on 15 June 1969. When Leavesden Flying School moved
into Panshanger during July 1969 to form the Panshanger Flying School, 'WSN was acquired for
providing tail wheel experience. The club was another short-lived venture and folded in 1970 with the
Condor moving to Portsmouth. The photograph was taken on 2 August 1970 during the Panshanger
Air Display. (Graham Lewis)

The Stampe SV-4C was Belgium's
answer to the Tiger Moth with
some improvements. This colourful
Belgian aerobatic aircraft was
operated by Ken Green and D.E.L.
McHarris from May 1969 and is
pictured outside the brick hangar.
On 15 May 1971 'XCZ force-
landed at Wareside after the engine
gave up during an aerobatic routine,
fortunately without injury to the
crew. It was later rebuilt and sold in
August 1975. (David P. Jones)

BARON AIR CHARTER

Another vision to promote general aviation and put Panshanger on the map came during July 1970 when Baron Air Charter, a Southend-based aircraft taxi and charter company, offered a flying taxi service from Luton or Panshanger to the north of England and the Continent. The service was aimed at the business traveller and stated boldly, 'Call a plane and forget about those costly traffic delays', requiring a prospective traveller to contact Baron Air Charter who would then provide a suitable aircraft within two hours of their call. A round trip to Birmingham and Manchester would cost £100 and if a Beech Baron aircraft was filled the cost would work out at £20 a head. A larger Beechcraft Queen Air or Bell JetRanger helicopter could also be hired. It is doubtful that the service was very successful as Panshanger headed slowly into decline, losing its CAA license to operate such services and *ab initio* training later.

CLANDESTINE OPERATIONS

In late April 1971 a Cessna 337 arrived overhead the Sir Frederic Osborn School and approached to land at Panshanger. Whilst this was not unusual as such, the aircraft type and the scenes afterwards were a talking point. The avid spotters amongst the school fraternity (myself included) watched the aircraft land and taxi to park. Within seconds wailing sirens of police cars echoed across the fields as a small force moved in to block the escape route of the plane and its occupants, for the unscheduled arrival had been a little more clandestine than a routine flight, the Cessna containing four illegal immigrants. The pilot, a Mr Osbourne, was later charged under the Commonwealth Immigrants Act.

Much later, on 18 June 1996, Panshanger saw the arrival of a Britten Norman Islander AL.1 of the Army Air Corps, ZG846, belonging to No.1 Flight Aldergrove, Northern Ireland. The aircraft was involved in undisclosed trials with a ground liaison vehicle (red Transit van!).

The first AJEP Wittman Tailwind, G-AYDU, was test-flown by Bill Bowker from Panshanger on 24 March 1972. G-AYDU was based on the airfield and converted later for trials on behalf of the Ministry of Defence. Andrew Perkins built a further two conventional Wittman Tailwinds at Panshanger until AJEP Developments sold the jigs. (David P. Jones)

AJEP DEVELOPMENTS

Around 1968 Andrew Perkins, a former Vauxhall Motors engineer and CAA approved welder, had built a single-seat Taylor Monoplane, G-AVPX, which was flown from Panshanger and Rush Green, near Hitchin, Hertfordshire. Andrew had a vision to construct a two-seat aircraft and offer kits for the fledgling home-build market in the United Kingdom. He chose a high wing American design, the Wittman Tailwind, and developed the W-8C version at Panshanger. The first UK-registered aircraft was G-AYDU and incorporated many design changes to enable easy construction and better performance. AJEP Developments was established to handle small-scale production at Panshanger with the construction undertaken at the Gate House in Panshanger Lane and the registered address of The Lodge, Marden Hill Farm. The first aircraft, G-AYDU, was based on the aerodrome and comprehensively tested by Neil Williams. G-AYDU was fitted later with a nose wheel for better ground handling and later still converted for pilot-less aircraft trials on behalf of the Ministry of Defence at RAE Llanbedr; however, the Ministry did not adopt the type. Andrew Perkins built a further two conventional Wittman Tailwinds at Panshanger, G-BALR and G-BCBR (registered in 1973 and 1974 respectively), but then sold the production jigs to the Whiting Brothers in Yorkshire, who constructed two more during 1975.

TRAGEDY – ONCE AGAIN

On 5 March 1973 an American pilot, Tileston Holland-Hale, was killed whilst flying his Bolkow Junior, G-ASFT, which crashed into trees near the aerodrome, the weather at the time being very inclement. The official report into the accident notes the pilot as being intoxicated prior to flying and performing highly dangerous manoeuvres in the air during which he evidently lost control in the low cloud and crashed.

The Bolkow 208 Junior was an all-metal aircraft designed in the USA during the late 1950s by Bjorn Andreasson and licence built in Germany from April 1962 by Bolkow Apparatebau GmbH. From July 1972 G-ASFT was based at Panshanger, being owned and flown by an American, Tileston Holland-Hale. On 5 March 1973, in marginal weather, the aircraft crashed within the aerodrome boundary, killing the pilot. (Richard Riding)

DEPRESSION

The late 1970s was a period of limbo for the aerodrome with the progressive encroachment of housing nibbling at the land. The loss of the CAA licence to operate training and provide other services led to a gradual decline over this period and the threat of eventual closure hung over the private aircraft hangared there. No flying training was allowed from Panshanger but a rich variety of private aircraft were still maintained, hangared on both north and south sides of the aerodrome. The aerodrome retained two grass runways, an east–west main runway (09-27) of approximately 1,167m and a shorter one (914m) north–south. This was an interesting affair with the approach from Tewin high over the Mimram Valley and the ground suddenly rushing up to meet you. The south end became unworkable with the ingress of housing and by the end of the decade the runway ceased to be.

Later in the decade the encroaching housing and closure of the north–south runway forced a change in the remaining east–west runway direction to 30-15 with appropriate marking.

The approach to runway 27 in 1977 viewed from Auster J-1 G-AIBX, showing the dilapidated London Aeroplane Club flight hut, left of centre. (Author)

An aerial view taken in the summer of 1977 showing the housing had reached Long Ley and the natural barrier of the realigned public bridleway. Springmead JMI School is to the left side. The north–south runway becomes untenable with the progressive development of housing after approvals for building in the early 1980s. Runway 270°/060° was moved to head 290°/110° by 1982, funnelling away from the housing. (Author)

Opposite below: Built by Reims Aviation in France, G-AVHM is a Cessna F150G and in this 1977 photograph leased by the Executive Flying Club from Municipal Products & Services Ltd for *ab initio* work. Flying instructor Ed James sits with David Oliver pending a flight. A transit flight to Leavesden had to be made to train officially since the aerodrome was unlicensed at this time. The Cessna was replaced by G-AVZU in 1978. (David Oliver)

Right: The aerodrome plan from 1977 showing the two
runways. (Author)

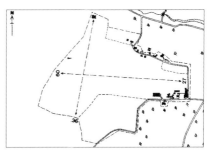

Below: A 1980 shot looking west over the aerodrome
showing the extent of housing up to the self-build at
Long Ley. Springmead JMI School is in the centre and
the municipal golf course to the right. The runway is
marked officially 300/120. (David Jones)

This Jodel D.11, G-BCGW, was registered in June 1974 to G.H. & M.D. Chittenden and built locally. It is seen at Panshanger in 1978 looking to all intents as a RAF 1950s training aircraft. The brothers moved the aircraft to Highwood Hall in 1979. (David Oliver)

This Piper PA-24 Comanche 260 was registered G-ATAO on 29 January 1965 and after a variety of owners it arrived at Elstree in April 1975 with Botsford & Sons (Builders) Ltd. It was based at Panshanger later and the photograph was taken in 1978. On 3 December 1981 'TAO ditched in the Channel, 30 miles off Bournemouth, and sank, fortunately without loss of life. (David P. Jones)

After serving with the RAF as WZ876, this de Havilland DHC-1 Chipmunk 22 was part of a large sale during 1972 and 1973 and registered G-BBWN on 11 January 1974. In July 1975 Colton Aviation Services acquired the aircraft and it was flown by Gerry Mead from Panshanger for several years. (David P. Jones)

Reims Aviation, France commenced licensed production of the Cessna F.172 in 1963 and the F.150 in 1965. Cessna F.150H G-AVZU was registered in December 1967 to Gregory Air services at Denham, moving to Stansted in August 1975. By 1977 it was based at Panshanger with the Executive Flying Club, run by Ed James, and used the blister hangar on the north site. The group had to carry out *ab initio* training from Leavesden due to the lack of licence at Panshanger, which meant plenty of cross-country work for circuits. The club moved to High Cross, near Ware, by October 1979. (Author)

The single-seat Jodel D.9 was designed for homebuilders and in this case powered by the ubiquitous Volkswagen air-cooled, flat four engine. G-AXYU was constructed by J.A. Littlechild and registered in March 1970, making its first flight from Panshanger later that year. It was purchased by David Jones in October 1978 but damaged at Clothall Common on 20 August 1979, necessitating a rebuild just off site at Warrengate Farm. Subsequently it moved to Old Warden and Little Gransden. (David P. Jones)

The all-metal, four-seat Omnipol L-40 Meta Sokol originated from Czechoslovakia powered by a 110hp M-332 piston engine. Immediately recognisable by its reversed tricycle undercarriage, two were imported in June 1959. 'PUE was registered to Retford Air Services who had received it under the Czech registration OK-NMB in April that year. After a couple more owners 'PUE arrived at Panshanger in July 1976 registered to Mr P. Phipps, owner of Broxbourne Zoo. Its conservative blue and white trim was converted into this bizarre concoction of shapes, symbols and scenes during the summer of 1977 by a young artist, commissioned by the new owner. When completed the aircraft languished in the north blister hangar after losing its C of A, following the owner leaving the scene after the enforced closure of his zoo due to breaches in health regulations. Thankfully 'PUE was rescued and moved to Bagby initially. It is now airworthy and based at Top Farm near Royston. (Author)

Opposite above: This Piper PA-23 Apache 160, G-ARJR, arrived at Panshanger in 1978 and had a short residency being damaged beyond economical repair in a forced landing near Little Berkhampstead, Hertfordshire, on 22 July 1978. It was dismantled and ended up at Kidlington, being used for instructional use. (David P. Jones)

Opposite below: The Evans VP-1 Volksplane was designed for amateur construction and G-BBXZ was built by G.D.M. Price at Shoreham during 1974. Transferred to Panshanger by 1978, it was badly damaged in a forced landing after engine failure on the approach to land in December that year. (David Oliver)

INCIDENTS

There were two further accidents to Panshanger aircraft during the decade. On 21 May 1978 Auster J/1 G-AJIU suffered a loss of power after a touch and go and the pilot made a forced landing in a ploughed field at Tewin, which unfortunately caused the aircraft to turn over. It was rebuilt later. On Boxing Day 1978 an Evans Volksplane, G-BBXZ, suffered the engine fail on finals and ended up force-landing at Potters Green causing substantial damage to the port wing and airframe.

HELICOPTERS

Autair helicopters moved their maintenance facilities from Luton in the mid-1970s and located the servicing in the old wartime training and lecture blocks. Autair had been formed by Bill Armstrong from an older helicopter concern, using the Bell 47. Autair became Trent Helicopters and during the 1980s Aeromega, undertaking helicopter maintenance and rebuilds over this period. Very exotic machines arrived at Panshanger and the remains of Ugandan Westland Scouts, Danish Sikorsky S-55s were resident for a number of years in the T2 hangar. Located here for a period in the 1980s was a Lockheed T-33 as well.

Taken at Panshanger on 27 May 1991 showing the clear-out of the helicopters owned by Autair/Trent and Aeromega. The Sikorsky S-55 was licensed-built in the UK by Westland Helicopters at Yeovil and known as the Whirlwind. The Autair example is a Silorsky S-55B, ZS-HDG, transferred from Luton in 1988 and stripped of parts. The machines are ex-Danish Air force S-55. (Dave Williams)

14

The 1980s & '90s

In December 1979 a press release mentioned that Nat Somers and the London Aeroplane Club Ltd had applied to the Civil Aviation Administration (CAA) for the aerodrome to be licensed for development into a general aviation base for advanced flying training, engineering and aircraft sales. Leavesden-based D.F. Aviation planned to move their flying school to Panshanger.

In January 1980 British Aerospace wrote to the CAA to express concerns over safety with Hatfield test flying and a prospective huge increase in Panshanger circuit traffic. The CAA agreed to the aerodrome being licensed providing there was mutual agreement between Hatfield, Panshanger and Luton Airport operations. British Aerospace was highly vocal on the matter and proposed restricted airspace at Panshanger and all operations from the aerodrome to receive prior clearance from Hatfield air traffic control.

The new CAA licence for D.F. Aviation to operate training concerned British Aerospace (BAe) management at Hatfield since they were becoming ever more active in development and production flying of the new BAe 146 regional airliner. This and the progressive development of the Hatfield Aerodrome during the 1980s into a centre for business flying resulted in the formalised reporting and approach procedure for pilots using Panshanger. The location of Hatfield Aerodrome's outer marker beacon, originally in the top north-west corner of the aerodrome, moved to Archers Green in the 1970s and caused the approach flight path of Hatfield-bound aircraft to come close to the circuit height of Panshanger traffic. Panshanger retained a 700' circuit for this reason and in the days of test flying by very experienced de Havilland, Hawker Siddeley and later British Aerospace test pilots there were no serious incidents. The same security could not be afforded by the general aviation that Aerospace was considering to expand and secure the future of the Hatfield site. British Aerospace provided a portacabin at Panshanger during the early 1980s to act as a control facility, providing a land-line telephone and VHF radio for BAe air traffic controllers. Panshanger VHF radio frequency was allocated as 120.25 MHz. The remaining east–west runway was moved in position and direction, to 120° – 300°, the whole lot shifted a little to the north to provide better approach and 'emergency procedures' as well as reduced noise for the encroaching housing. This alteration reduced the length somewhat and the direction meant emergency procedures were not for the faint-hearted.

PANSHANGER SCHOOL OF FLYING

The rapidly diminishing size of the aerodrome during the 1980s and the loss of facilities did not reduce the demand for flying training and the Panshanger School of Flying was formed in May 1982 by Alan Adams and Ian McLelland, following a renewal of the CAA licence. The club operated the Piper Tomahawk trainer throughout the remaining years of the aerodrome's history.

Panshanger School of Flying occupied two Handcraft huts on the south site (buildings No.57 and No.58). This photograph is dated 1987. (Mike Yalden)

The Partenavia P.68B Victor was a light twin touring aircraft for club use and G-BHJS arrived at Panshanger in December 1984 for J. Crook of Tewin Aviation, being used for twin engine conversion by the Panshanger School of Flying. It was sold to Sound Technology in April 1991 and moved away later. (Grant Peerless)

THE ROT SETS IN

An aerial photograph of the aerodrome from May 1980 begins to show a slow decay with partial collapse of the control building and fire damage to the maintenance hangar.

Later in the decade this hangar revealed Tiger Moth and Hornet Moth parts, probably transferred from the north site. These were salvaged during 1985 before the inevitable destruction occurred. The control building donated the original London Aeroplane Club Flight board to the Mosquito Museum at Salisbury Hall (de Havilland Aircraft Museum Trust). This revealed registration markings for Tiger Moths owned by the London Aeroplane Club when based at Hatfield, evidently a pre-war item.

A long-standing Panshanger resident is Piper PA-28R Cherokee Arrow 200, G-BBDE. It arrived for Robert Coleman in December 1985 and had to move to Stapleford Tawney in April 1992 when the airfield closed. It returned in November 1993 and was subsequently re-sprayed and, recently, fitted with a three-blade propeller. The photograph was taken on 20 April 1997. (Author)

The Allan-Williams turret found during the construction of the self-build homes in Long Ley and donated to the Panshanger School of Flying. (Mike Yalden)

During the construction of the self-build houses in Long Ley, bordering the footpath on the western edge of the aerodrome an Allan-Williams turret was removed to allow drainage to be dug. The turret was a prefabricated steel cupola designed for one soldier armed with a machine gun to defend the aerodrome. The top could be rotated through 360° for an all-round field of fire. A second turret was found on the northern part of the aerodrome guarding approaches there. The Long Ley turret was re-buried and the dome presented to Panshanger School of Flying.

On 13 March 1981 Peter Woods, of Elstree, was seriously hurt after crash-landing at Panshanger in Tiger Moth G-ALND, painted in wartime Royal Navy colours as N9191. The Tiger Moth suffered engine failure after take-off and stalled, crashing onto the runway.

ALL HOT AIR

In March 1986 the W.H. Review announced that Airship Industries would operate a single Skyship 500 from the aerodrome, carrying five passengers at £100 a time on a seventy-five-minute sightseeing tour of London, beginning on 23 April. The scheme ended on 31 May.

TOMAHAWK TRAGEDY

A serious accident occurred on 13 December 1986 when a Tomahawk G-BLKX of the School of Flying crashed into the wall of a house in St John's Road, Walthamstow, whilst attempting to make an emergency landing. The pilot, Elaine Fraser, had reported burning in the cockpit and attempted to land in a nearby field. Unfortunately, in the ensuing crash Elaine was injured and her passenger, Louise Sharp, of Welwyn Garden City, killed.

CHEROKEE CRASH

On 18 April 1991 a Piper Cherokee G-BJCJ owned by Wilsam Ltd departed Cambridge en route to Panshanger. The pilot was reported by Air Traffic at Cambridge for behaving erratically and the aircraft flew past Panshanger only to crash with fatal results in Prior Drive, Stanmore. Investigators found an empty bottle of vodka in the cockpit.

CLOSURE AND DESTRUCTION

The School of Flying continued to operate from the aerodrome and recorded 15,000 flights during 1987. The increasing spiral of rent charges and the general recession eventually forced the club to vacate the premises by April 1992 and move to Leavesden. The School of Flying was quoted as stating charges had reached £48,000 per year. Private owners complained that extremely high hangar rent charges forced them to look for premises elsewhere, such as Stapleford, Fowlmere, North Weald, Little Gransden and Elstree. The telephone land-line link went unanswered, control 'portacabin' vacated and the skies quietened to aircraft. Those that could not fly were transported by road from the site. The aerodrome leaseholders, P.S. Webber, were unavailable for comment, it appeared. It took very little time for the aerodrome to be inhabited by rather unwelcome guests in the form of gypsies, who arrived in caravans and ravaged all the remaining buildings for useable items and fuel. It took a lot longer to remove them and secure the site from further vandalism though sporadic fires and wanton damage reoccurred.

15

1993 Revival – East Herts Flying Club

A further revival of the aerodrome occurred in 1993 when Haim Merkado sought permission from the CAA to operate a licensed base for aircraft training, engineering and sales. Again there was intense opposition from British Aerospace, Hatfield, but the cruel irony of the parent aerodrome and factory closure left the way clear for Panshanger to become a licensed aerodrome again.

By June 1993, the grass runway was being cut and prepared for a lone Piper Tomahawk, G-DTOO, to arrive.

The old control building was in a dangerous state and soon demolished to clear the way for a larger parking area. Occupying the old lecture block, the East Herts Flying Club was formed by Haim Merkado to operate from Panshanger in flying training and club work and gradually worked up through the year, gaining a second Tomahawk and Cessna 150 later. Several former resident aircraft returned to the aerodrome during 1994, without the benefit of hangarage but with the security of the flying club and licensed facilities. The runway now lies heading 110°/290° with circuits away from the housing, the closest of which is some 100m or so from the track.

East Herts Flying School, Panshanger Aerodrome, Nr Hertford, SG14 2NH:

Equipment: (2006) – Various owners.

Piper Super Cub =	(G-BIDJ)
Piper Cherokee =	(G-BCGI, G-BEEU, G-BZWG)
Piper Archer =	(G-BMSD, G-BOOF, G-BWPH)
Piper Saratoga =	(G-BMJA)
Cessna 150/152 =	(G-BRBH, N4770B)
Grob G-115	(G-GROE)
Pitts S2A 2 =	(G-HISS)
Extra 300L	(D-ETTO)
Robinson R-22	(G-CDED)
Robinson R-44	(G-OBSM)
Aerospatiale Gazelle	(G-MANN)
Eurocopter EC.120D	(G-TBLY)

Haim Merkado formed the club in 1993 after he leased the aerodrome from Nat Somers. During its relatively short life the number of aircraft using the aerodrome as a base has

Registered new on 17 February 1979 as G-DTOO, this Piper PA-38 Tomahawk is credited as the first aircraft to arrive following the reopening of the aerodrome in June 1993. 'DTOO lasted until 9 July 1994 when it hit a fence at Seething, Norfolk, and was damaged beyond repair. (Author)

East Herts Flying School commenced operations in the summer of 1993 using the original lecture block building #65. This has been progressively improved internally and now boasts a restaurant, outdoor patio, seating area and large fish pond. (Grant Peerless)

This very rare Curtiss Robin C-2, G-HFBM, was registered in the UK on 24 April 1990 and is now owned by local resident David Forshaw, based primarily at High Cross but a frequent visitor for checks and maintenance. (Author)

Undergoing some engine work in June 1996, MS.880B Rallye Club, G-AYKF, was based at Panshanger for a mere four months until it was involved in a fatal accident after take-off from Barton, Manchester on 28 August 1996. The aircraft suffered engine failure and plunged into the ground killing the two occupants. (Author)

A vintage aircraft still resident at Panshanger is the delightful Tipsy Trainer, G-AFSC (11), owned by David Forshaw. The two-seat side-by-side trainer was designed by E.O. Tips and built initially by Avions Fairey SA in Belgium. Tipsy Aircraft Co. Ltd was established at Hanworth and later Slough, producing thirteen Trainers before the war, including 'FSC. Its first owner was the Airwork Flying Club at Heston in July 1939 and after the war it travelled extensively with various owners around the UK. It arrived at Panshanger in May 2000 and was photographed on 16 May 2002. (Author)

This Boeing A75-N1 Stearman served with the US Navy during the war as Bureau of Air No.43281 and was sold in Kenya later as VP-KRR. In August 1967 it was imported into the UK and flew for a while carrying registration 5Y-KRR until G-AWLO was allotted in June 1968, being registered to M T. Hynett. It was stored at Blackbushe, unconverted for civil use in the UK until restored to Doug Arnold in November 1978. It was acquired by local resident Nigel Pickard in the 1980s and based until forced away by the closure in 1992. Since the reopening of the aerodrome the Stearman has been a frequent visitor in summer months and highly distinctive in sound and vision. (Author)

This highly decorative Aerotek Pitts S2A Special, G-HISS, has been based at Panshanger since October 1994, registered then to Susan Byers and Haim Mercado. It was previously registered SE-GTX and G-BLVU. It is operated as the 'Pitts Experience' to enable anyone with a strong-enough constitution to savour the delights of aerobatic flying. G-HISS is now registered to Lance Adams and John Maffia. (Author)

Built by Canadian Car and Foundry, this Hawker Hurricane XII, G-HURR, made an impromptu
stop at Panshanger on 11 October 1997 after engine problems necessitated a precautionary landing en
route to Breighton in Yorkshire. All was sorted in a few days and the Hurricane went on its way on
15 October. (Author)

Taken at Panshanger on 18 June 1996 showing a visiting Pilatus Britten Norman BN-2T
Islander AL.1, ZG846, (ex G-BLNU) of No.1 Flight Army Air Corps based at Aldergrove.
This aircraft arrived from Shawbury and was involved in special operations with the
attending red van. It departed for Shawbury later. (Graham Lewis)

Heli-Air operated a small helicopter training facility at Panshanger, rotating various two-seat R-22 and four-seat R-44 between Denham and Wellesbourne Mountford. R-22 G-TOLY is seen here on 12 April 2003. (Author)

Sign at the entrance to the aerodrome (April 2006). (Author)

increased from one to upwards of thirty-five and the instructors from just Haim to ten others. Operations have changed too and training on single-engine aircraft has progressed to charter and training on multi-engine types, maintenance on customers' aircraft and, with the arrival in 1996 of Heli-Air, helicopter training as well. Heli Air used the small and demanding two-seat Robinson R-22 and its larger brother, the four-seat R-44. More recently the regular R-22 is now operated by A.D. Bly Leasing and the four-seat R-44 by Flight Solutions Ltd.

Haim acquired a two-seat Pitts Special biplane in 1996 and started the 'Pitts Experience' allowing the school to offer aerobatic training. This writer experienced the Pitts for himself and in short it is an experience never to be forgotten, despite the arrival on terra firma with an expression the same colour as the bright green of the aircraft.

More recently the East Herts Flying School changed its operating name to the North London Flying School.

The aerodrome receives many interesting aircraft, notably Nigel Pickard's Boeing Stearman biplane, David Forshaw's rare Curtiss Robin and Tipsy Trainer.

Recently the school celebrated its first ten years of operation with a spirited flying display and, after dark, a thrilling firework show. During 2004 the aerodrome attracted several aerobatic aircraft, the latest being Jason Newburg's American-registered Extra EA.230 and an example of its bigger brother, a two-seat Extra EA.300L.

The club provides a very friendly environment for the local public visitors too and is keen to work to preserve a harmony between the inevitable noise and activity in what is for an aerodrome, close proximity to the large expanse of housing at Panshanger. The club recently opened a Bistro café, named appropriately the Blue Skies Café. The web-site address for the school is www.northlondonflyingschool.com

GRAVEL EXTRACTION AND MORE HOUSING

Despite the continued operation of the aerodrome, the time will inevitably come when the value of the land outweighs its use for such luxuries as flying. Rumours of the local council's desire to investigate suitable areas for gravel extraction, housing and worse, landfill proliferate. The *Welwyn Hatfield Times* reported such in February 2002 and local area opposition groups were set up to challenge the proposals. Twenty-one sites in the local area were being investigated and these were short-listed to six around June 2002

ACCIDENTS

Several changes of resident aircraft have occurred over the period of operation and at least three Piper Tomahawks damaged in incidents. On 7 October 1995 G-BSOV was landing on runway 29 in a slight crosswind when it veered off into newly ploughed ground, removing the nosewheel and causing the aircraft to turn over. Fortunately both passengers were unhurt though the Tomahawk suffered terminal disfigurement. G-BSVV suffered a hard landing on 29 May and was repaired later. On 2 June 1996 during climb out G-BSKC suffered an engine misfire and the instructor put the aircraft down in a field near Moss Bank Farm, Tewin. The crew was unhurt and the Tomahawk later dismantled and stored on the aerodrome. It was removed during 1997.

April 1996 saw the arrival of a French Rallye aircraft, G-AYKF, which was flown regularly during the late spring. Sadly on 26 August 1996 the aircraft crashed on take-off from Barton, Manchester, killing the pilot, Turkish sports journalist Ender Erturan, and passenger Younus Agaoglu.

Recently (2003) there have been two accidents on the aerodrome, fortunately without injuries. On 1 March resident Cherokee Six, G-RAYE, slid off the end of runway 29 and damaged its undercarriage and port wing, while Tomahawk G-BSVV was in the wars again, this time losing its nosewheel in a heavy landing on 15 March. Both aircraft have since been written-off.

The use of the aerodrome as an aerodrome is welcomed by most residents of the Panshanger estate since it restricts further development for a while, provides a source of relaxation and entertainment and a chance to fly for modest cost in comparison with other nearby flying clubs. The aerodrome retains a quiet charm and sense of history, despite the ever-increasing foliage masking the old and dilapidated buildings that still exist. And long may it remain so.

On 1 March 2003 Piper Cherokee Six, G-RAYE, slid off the end of runway 29 after returning to Panshanger from Humberside and was severely damaged, fortunately without injury to the solo pilot. 'RAYE arrived at Panshanger in August 2000, registered to Gordon Silver of the G-RAYE Group, but was written-off after the accident. (Terry Pole)

Recent photograph of the aerodrome showing Nick Richards' Extra 300L D-ETTO, resident since March 2004, and the Pitts S-2A, G-HISS. (Grant Peerless)

Appendices

Brief History of the Reserve Flying School (de Havilland)

The Reserve Flying School operated originally under contract by commercial companies and their functions varied from time to time but essentially they provided Reservists of the Royal Air Force opportunity to put in their annual hours of flying, so-called 'refresher' flying. The Reserve Flying School's history stems back to 1 April 1923 when the de Havilland School of Flying was appointed as No.1 Reserve School for the RAF to provide training being based at Stag Lane Aerodrome in Edgware. The school moved to Hatfield in June 1930 and thence to Holwell Hyde/Panshanger by 1943.

In the early days aircraft included the venerable DH.9 and DH.9J, supplemented by the DH.60 Moth from 1925, Gipsy Moth (1929) and DH.82A Tiger Moth (1930). House colours were adopted for all schools and the de Havilland School of Flying used deep red for fuselage and struts with silver-doped wings and tailplane (originally gold!). These were heady days before the war and all aircraft operated under civilian registration; however, from 1935 onward world events became increasingly grave and the reserve schools became responsible for the elementary training of all officer and airmen pilots entering the RAF on short-term commissions. Annual flying time was increased to encompass all aspects of Service flying training and continuous courses for twenty to thirty pupils of fifty hours' training in eight weeks prior to entering a Service training school became the standard practice. The civilian aspect of the training course was dropped and the de Havilland School of Flying became 1 ERFTS (Elementary & Reserve Flying Training School) on 4 August 1935 and 1 EFTS on 3 September 1939, under 50 Group, as a Class 'B' unit.

Class	Pupils	Flights	Aircraft	(Initial Establishment/Immediate Reserve)
C	60	Two	24	12
B	90	Three	36	18
A	120	Four	48	24
A + 1	150	Five	60	30
A + 2	180	Six	72	36

The formation of the Volunteer Reserve in 1937 necessitated the need for up-to-date Service aircraft and the Hawker Hart and Hind were employed initially and later, just before the war, the Fairey Battle. The Avro Anson was used for navigational and radio (wireless) training.

Whilst the parent base at this time was Hatfield, the school had use of a Reserve Landing Ground at Sandridge. This landing ground was situated to the west of the village on a hill to the south-west of Hillend Farm and rumoured to have been used for storage of factory-fresh de Havilland Mosquitoes during the war, pending their delivery to units.

At the outbreak of the war the school had course entrants for short service commissions, these being completed by October 1939. A few weeks later volunteer reserve refresher training commenced and by the end of 1939 the first two war courses arrived at Hatfield, of forty-five pupils each, remaining with the school for five months (this was the 'phoney war' period). The Training School followed a set organisation under the auspices of 50 Group Royal Air Force. Schools were classified on size and from the outbreak of the war 1 EFTS was noted as Class B.

The EFTS came under full RAF control on 1 January 1940. After Dunkirk in May 1940, training was speeded up considerably and by 1 January 1941 the school had grown to Class A. By June 1941 the school had 180 pupils on strength and by the fourteenth of the month was reclassified Class A + 1. Long-course training continued until grading was introduced in 1941 with the first course commencing in September. That same month the Central Link Trainer Flight was attached to 1 EFTS, becoming 'L' Flight, equipped with four Proctor aircraft and one in reserve. Initially the Flight was located at Hatfield and moved to Panshanger on 15 August 1943, remaining part of 1 EFTS until 10 October 1944.

Numbers under training reduced gradually during 1942 and by 1 June the school was classed C again. The move of 'B' Flight to Holwell Hyde is described elsewhere and the eventual transfer of the entire school in September 1942 was less of a 'numbers game' since the Commonwealth training plan had been inaugurated and transferred a large part of RAF training overseas.

The first of several Air Observation Post (AOP) courses started in 1942, using the ubiquitous Tiger Moth with additional Auster Mk.I aircraft. Elementary flying training for a variety of services was provided. The first complete Dutch fighter squadron was trained at 1 EFTS, a course for Turkish officers, short courses for Royal Navy senior officers, junior Canadian Navy officers and elementary training for glider pilots and MoS (Ministry of Supply) technicians were completed. Honours for its students included one MBE, six AFC, one AFM, three commendations for valuable service and three certificates for good service. During the six years of war more than 4,800 students passed through, with an additional 1,000 Link Trainer instructors given a short course on Proctor aircraft. Some 550 overseas-trained pilots were given acclimatisation courses as well. With the end of the war the inevitable rundown began and by 15 August 1945 the school had reduced in size to thirty aircraft.

The EFTS transferred to 23 Group charge on 21 April 1947 and became 1 RFS on 5 May 1947 under the direct guidance of the de Havilland Aeronautical Technical School, continuing its role with the Tiger Moth in providing training for pilots and engineers alike. On 1 April 1948 the school completed twenty-five years of service, continuing under the auspices of the de Havilland Aircraft Co. During the summer of 1950 the Reserve Flying School began to supplement the Tiger Moth with the Chipmunk trainer, in addition to using the twin-engine Anson as flying classrooms for navigators. 1 RFS transferred to 61 Group charge 1 February 1951.

Prior to Christmas 1952 the Air Ministry announced the end of the Reserve Flying Schools by 31 March 1953, and thirty years after it opened, the school closed and aircraft were dispersed.

A poignant reminder as to the destiny of the airfield at Panshanger was made in the *de Havilland Gazette* for April 1953. C. Martin Sharpe's words:

> With the demise of 1 RFS it becomes more than ever important that the other de Havilland centre of training; the London Aeroplane Club, should be kept alive in the face of the odds which threaten it and the light aeroplane movement as a whole, in these difficult times.

APPENDIX 2

Housing Development

The airfield was conceived in 1940 to act as a decoy field, far enough away from local civilisation to avoid possible casualties during an enemy attack. Its later use as an airfield proper has been explained in the text; however, the proximity to Welwyn Garden City and the plans for town expansion were bound to conflict with the coming of peace. Indeed prior to the start of the war Welwyn Garden City Urban District Council (WGCUDC) had been purchasing land in the area for just this purpose; the eastern area of the town earmarked for housing.

Examples of this were:

24 March 1933	22½ acres Black Fan area sold.
26 July 1938	½ acre at Cole Green
19 December 1939	¼ acre Welwyn – Hertford road at Tewin
12 June 1940	Part of Herns Wood, Tewin
21 June 1940	Twenty perches Hertford – Welwyn road at Tewin
21 June 1940	Hertford to Burnham Green Road widening
12 May 1941	16½ acres at Black Fan
19 November 1946	One rod eight perches Black Fan junction at WGC

In July 1972 fears about the future of the airfield were heightened by the owners of the London Aeroplane Club submitting proposals to the WGC Urban District Council seeking planning permission to use some airfield land for housing. On each of the three occasions planning was refused due to the land being designated inside the green belt. In that month the Hertfordshire Flying Association was set up by the owners of private aircraft based at Panshanger, to lobby County Planning authorities in an attempt to designate the area as an airfield on future consultative maps and documents. By then half the land occupied was in the green belt and the remainder 'an area of outstanding natural beauty'. Welwyn Rural District Council recognised the need and support for an airfield in the area but stated that its objectors felt the airfield owner was frustrating this support by pressing for its development into housing. (*WHT* 28 July 1972). The Association's concerns were alleviated a little during 1973, when the London Aeroplane Club's chairman sought planning permission again but was refused by both the council and the Department of the Environment.

During the latter half of 1979 the chairman, Nat Somers, sought the go-ahead for a £20 million housing development with 500 to 600 homes planned on a 62-acre site occupying one-third of the existing airfield (Moneyhole Lane area and adjoining land to the north). One factor aiding the application concerned the acute shortage of housing in the district. Land outside the airfield boundary owned by the New Towns Commission had been sold up to this date and built on by developers. The last parcel of this, 43 acres, was sold during the early part of 1980 and construction of housing passed to the hands of developers.

In December 1979 Leavesden-based D.F. Aviation made known their intention to move to Panshanger with fourteen aircraft to operate a flying training school and air taxi service on the proviso that permission for the latest housing development was the end of the matter. Despite heated objections from British Aerospace at Hatfield, a new operating licence was granted and the Panshanger School of Flying began training in 1982, whilst continued planning applications stumbled on.

By June 1981 further proposals by the London Aeroplane Club sought planning permission for a 20-acre site running the length of the back gardens at Long Ley and a 40-acre site with a boundary just north of the junction of Hardings and Long Ley. Protests from Panshanger estate residents and pilots alike reached the Welwyn Hatfield Council and the plan was shelved since the proposed site would have encroached onto the existing airfield and forced a further alteration in the runway layout, causing aircraft to come very close to the Springmead School. The new site was zoned inside the green belt as an airfield in the county 'blueprint', 'Hertfordshire 1981'. (*WHT*, 26 June 1981). The heat died down a while but public concern over future housing proposals returned during November 1981 with the Community Association at Panshanger objecting to the 20-acre development and its expected problems from more residents requiring more of the paucity of services and children's play areas. Some 46 acres of land at Moneyhole Lane (the original decoy airfield site) was allocated as public open space with facilities for football, allotments, a play area, car park and bridleway (which last was already there). If this land was not used then another 20 acres of land of outstanding natural beauty would be. The runway would be re-aligned so as not to inconvenience existing residents or schools. (*WHT*, 13 November 1981).

During the last quarter of 1982 the granting of an operating licence by the CAA initiated a few changes to the airfield boundary with a large fence being erected to prevent misguided wanderings across the active airfield runway. By this time the north–south bridleway marked the western boundary of housing, particularly in the area of Long Ley (self-build housing) (*WHT*, 12 November 1982). The gradual wearing down of objections to the housing continued and by 1985 further plans for 900 homes were revealed by London Mercantile Holdings who applied for permission to develop 65 acres of the 80-acre site over the following seven years. The company had received the go-ahead for 20 acres to be developed already (those mentioned during 1981). This land crossed the western boundary for the first time and extended from Moors Walk, north along Bericot Way to Wellington Drive and on to what is now Lysander Way. In addition the New Towns Commission owned 18 acres to the west of the bridleway, north-west of the currently unfinished roundabout on Bericot and Lysander Way, the land adjacent to Springmead School, which would contain 250 homes. In October 1985 permission to build here was refused since houses would stand too close to the runway which, it was claimed, could not be moved as far as first thought. Until now this land has been allowed to lie fallow. A spokesman for the developers, Bovis Homes, stated that the airfield would 'continue to operate normally' following house building and by June 1985 had received the necessary permission for development to begin during the spring of 1986.

Currently the final phase of the 65-acre development is complete, with the airfield boundaries marked in the west by the bridleway, to the north by Warrengate Farm, the original 1944 eastern boundary footpath and the south by the houses adjacent to Lysander and Halifax Way.

On 17 December 1987, some eighteen months later, the local newspaper reported that rumours of the imminent closure of the airfield to make room for more housing were unfounded. The airfield manager, Alan Adams, went further, unveiling plans to develop 50,000ft^2 of the site with two new hangars, a mini control tower and offices. Panshanger airfield reported 15,000 flights during 1987. Suffice it to say the airfield was not developed further but did remain operational for another five years.

The large-scale development of housing in the Panshanger area ended in 1993 and the airfield has remained active since this time under the constraints of the council's policy plans. Recent desires to use the land for gravel extraction (an extension of the current work across Panshanger Lane to the old estate site) has created public reaction to the move. It remains to be seen whether the land is safe from this plan, which will inevitably bring to an end the period of flying from Panshanger.

The Welwyn Hatfield Council plan for 2001 remains:

> There is a remaining active airfield in the District at Panshanger, which was formerly a military airfield but granted planning permission as a civil airfield in 1954 (sic) for use by light aircraft. Since then the Panshanger residential area has been developed and now borders the airfield. The airfield is identified in the Plan as an area of special restraint and has been since

1993. This means that it has been safeguarded for potential future development needs in the district beyond the period of this Plan. As such its release for development will be a matter for consideration in a future review of the Plan.

Meanwhile, there are increasing concerns about the effect of aircraft noise from the airfield on residents in Panshanger and surrounding villages. The Council will therefore continue to monitor its use to ensure that it is being operated within the terms of its planning permission and within acceptable noise levels on the ground. However, the Council cannot act against aircraft in flight. The Civil Aviation Authority (CAA) regulates controlled airspace, but general aviation, such as the light aircraft using Panshanger, fall outside those controls. The CAA would only become involved if heavier aircraft were to use the airfield. The Council will not permit any expansion of facilities or intensification of the use of the airfield beyond the limits of the existing planning permission.

June 2002 – Policy GBSP3 – Area of Special Restraint and Structural Landscape Area.

The 1993-adopted District Plan identified such an area of land, designated as an Area of Special Restraint, at Panshanger Aerodrome on the eastern edge of Welwyn Garden City. In preparing this Review, the Council has given consideration to whether this land should be released to meet development requirements in the period up to 2011. The Council is satisfied that these requirements can be accommodated on the sites identified within the towns and settlements elsewhere in the Plan. However, in order to maintain the permanence of the Green Belt this Area of Special Restraint has been retained and will be safeguarded to allow space for the development needs of the area beyond the Plan period. This land is not required for the development in the period up to 2011. Its release for development after 2011 will be a matter for consideration in future reviews of the Plan, in the light of longer-term development requirements and advice on the sequential selection of land for development contained in government guidance. Should this land be released for development in the longer term an area of land on its northern edge has been identified for structural landscaping to be provided in advance of any development to minimise its impact on the surrounding landscape and long distance views

APPENDIX 3

The Buildings – Past and Present

The decoy site has been outlined earlier and suffice it to say nothing remains of this facility other than the land it once occupied is still undeveloped for housing, remaining an area for recreation as Moneyhole Lane Park, Panshanger.

The Air Ministry Plan for Panshanger (PR187) is dated 1944, with amendments made in 1952.

The site is best divided into two main parts. Appendix 3a covers the buildings in more specific detail.

The North Site

Developed for the initial location of 1 EFTS ('B' Flight), access being via Warrengate Farm from the B1000. Two 69ft-wide Miskin Extra Over blisters (32 and 75) were ready by November 1942 with up to five 45ft wood-framed Miskin standards (able to handle a single Tiger Moth each) to complement the steel-framed hangars. There is little evidence of the wooden-framed hangars after 1943 but since they were readily transportable this is not surprising.

Hangar 72 was erected for 'B' Flight and tucked into the north-west corner. Although 45ft in width, it appears to have been twice the length of a standard blister and lasted until 1953 when, after the closure of 1 RFS, it was dismantled.

Hangar 74 on the 1944 plan might be a relocation of an earlier blister. 74 or a similarly positioned steel-framed hangar lasted until July 1980 when it caught fire one night whilst housing a Robin DR.400 aircraft.

Hangar 75 was built for 'L' Flight, the Link Trainer Flight and remains a stark and naked steel frame denuded of the corrugated steel cladding after being withdrawn from active use after 1953.

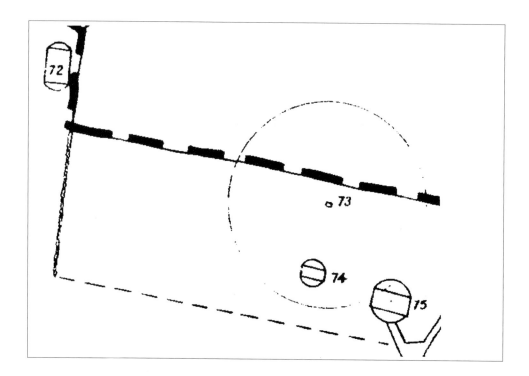

North-West Site

Key

72	Blister Hangar 'B' Flight
73	Incendiary, Bomb & Component Store
74	Blister Hangar 45ft 'L' Flight
75	Blister Hangar 69ft 'L' Flight

Crown Copyright, RAF Museum.

Crown Copyright material is reproduced with the permission of the Controller of Her Majesty's Stationery Office.

Moving to the right the main north site was as follows:

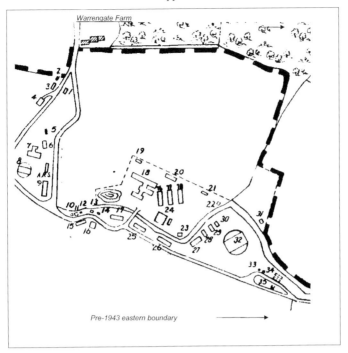

Warrengate Farm

Pre-1943 eastern boundary ⟶

North Site

Key

1	Guard House	22	Destructor Horsfall Type
2	Link Trainer Store	23	Armoury
3	Link Trainer	24	Coke Compound
4	Petrol Installation, Aviation	25	Barrack Hut (for six)
5	Latrines	26	Barrack Hut (for ten)
6	Coke Compound	27	Ration Store
7	Gas Defence Centre	28	NFE Store
8	MT Storage 45ft Blister Hangar	29	AMWD Store
9	'L' Flight Hut	30	Station Contractors Store
10	'B' Flight Store	31	Sewage Disposal Works
11	'B' Flight Locker Room	32	Blister Hangar 69ft 'B' Flight
12	Fire Pool Hut	33	Lubricating Oil Tanks two 500 gal
13	Dope Store	34	Petrol Installation, Aviation two 12,000 gal
14	Latrines	35	Petrol Installation, MT two 500 gal
15	'B' Flight Hut	76	Barrack Hut for ten (April 1951)
16	MT Shed	77	Barrack Hut for ten
17	Clothing Store	78	Barrack Hut for ten
18	RAF Mess		
19	Drying Room & Latrine		
20	Baths & Ablutions Block		
21	Latrines		

The access road through the farm rises quite steeply from the Mimram Valley. Buildings 1–3 are still in evidence and located on the farmland. The original petrol installation (4) and latrines (5) are still present. Building 6 – Hangar 8 are all gone. Hangar 8 (Miskin 45ft standard) was probably present from the earliest days, being used for MT (Motor Transport) storage until vacated by the London Aeroplane Club in 1953. Being wood framed it did not fair well afterwards. Debris from it can still be seen in dense undergrowth.

Reference should be made to the decoy site map that shows the many runways.

Moving the runways during 1943 would have meant that some original hangars became awkwardly placed and the extra hangarage available on the south site had by then reduced the need. It is possible that another wooden blister stood in a similar place prior to building the 'B' flight hut (15). The attendant services and storage huts were ready by the end of 1941, including stores (10), latrines (14), flight hut (15), clothing store (17) and barracks (25), the latter replacing tented accommodation. The barracks survived until the late 1980s.

Mention must be made of the low grass bank that now secludes the former access road from the current airfield. This was constructed during the early 1980s, marking the border of land and buildings transferred to Warrengate farmland, and roughly follows a line west of the petrol installation to the start of the road. It then makes a ridge south of the road until the road turns into the Mess area. Buildings 15 and MT garage 16 remained on the airfield. The ridge isolated the 1954 London Aeroplane Club hangar (not on the map) that was purchased by the Barton family for farm use. On the western end of this hangar was a brick workshop, which became a pig-rearing pen, as well as housing David Jones' Jodel D.9 (G-AXYU), under repair during the early 1980s.

The access road from the B1000 to the north site, through Warrengate Farm, was called Moneyhole Lane, an old farm track that crossed the arable land and joined Green Lane to the south of the site. Moneyhole Lane divided in the area of Bericot Green (the main area of the north site) and a second track ran east towards the Henry Wood – B1000 footpath. There was a natural elbow in the route and hangar 32 was built in this slight dip, together with the RAF Mess (18), attendant latrines, ablutions and coal storage to the north of the track. The three Seco (wood) barrack huts added by 1951 for ten men each (76–78) are located in the Mess compound and still exist, having been sold into private use after the closure of the RFS.

Hangar 32 remains intact and was used for aircraft storage until closure in 1992. This was a 'B' flight facility, later used for Ansons and later still (1955) for storage of ex-RAF

The denuded Miskin blister hangar still sits on the north site, formerly used by 1 EFTS and the London Aeroplane Club until 1953 when it was stripped of corrugated panels which were used to complete a smaller blister hangar on the south site, built over the old coal store. (Author)

The motor transport (MT) shed is largely complete though
succumbing to the vegetation. By the early 1980s an earth bank was
added to separate the aerodrome from Warrengate Farm and this
runs to the right of this 1993 photograph. (Author)

Proctors. In the early 1960s Keegan Aviation used the hangar and several spare parts for the
Canadair C-4M were found there many years later. Behind this hangar were two Nissen
huts and other buildings. One Nissen survives and the barrack huts are now occupied,
being on private land.

The aircraft oil and petrol facility (33–35) is now under felled trees. The area was
relatively intact until recently, being hidden under dense undergrowth. A small spur off
the main track is the delivery route to the underground fuel storage where two 12,000-
gallon fuel tanks were placed in troughs with the valves and pipework, though rusting, still
present. It is likely this facility supplemented that visible at point 4 on the map once the
site expanded in 1943. Oil and fuel fed MT and aircraft via a pumping station. A pipeline
runs above the ground towards the airmens' quarters, which are now private dwellings
and should not be approached without permission. Oil storage tanks are still visible near
the fuelling depot.

Prior to the opening of the south site in 1943 the airfield's eastern border was along a track
bordering a north–south hedgerow extending from Hangar 32 down to the trees of Henry
Wood. The track then ran west to the old corner, and down to the decoy site. Following
the setting of the four runways by late 1941, Moneyhole Lane was no longer a suitable track
and had been 'stopped up' in 1945 under Defence Regulation 16, which prevented its use by
farmers. When the airfield entered private hands after 1953 the track was redirected to the
western boundary, becoming a footpath later in the decade. Another minor farm track to the
north-west ceased to be used as well.

After the opening of the south site a new concrete perimeter road ran east from Hangar
32 to the natural border of the bridleway. Along this road was the compass base, which is just
visible in winter.

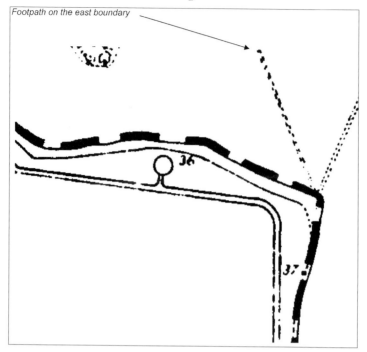

North-East Site

Key

36 Compass Base
37 Ammunition Store
Crown Copyright, RAF Museum.
Crown Copyright material is reproduced with the permission of the Controller of Her Majesty's Stationery Office

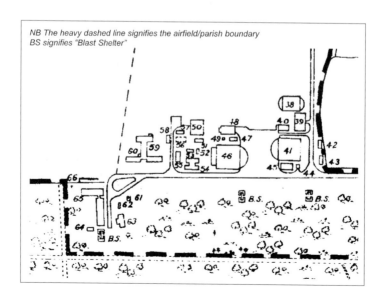

The South Site

The main south site was built from late 1942 until summer 1943 on a new portion of the land to the east of the original hedgerow which was almost completely removed to gain access to the new facilities. Three blast shelters remain in Henry Wood; ostensibly for the station staff after the decoy facility was dismantled.

BS signifies 'Blast Shelter'.

Crown Copyright, RAF Museum.

Crown Copyright material is reproduced with the permission of the Controller of Her Majesty's Stationery Office.

Key

38	Blister Hangar three 45ft Combined		58	Instructors Rest & Locker Room
39	Coke Compound		59	Station HQ & Watch Tower
40	Lubricant & Inflammable Store		60	Switch House
41	Blister Hangar Storage two 69ft		61	Sub Station
42	Guard Sleeping Quarters		62	Latrines
43	Main Guard Hut		63	Link Trainer
44	Fire Pool Hut		64	Library
45	Static Water 30,000 gallons		65	Lecture Block
46	Blister Hangar & Annex		66	Sleeve Streamer Mast
47	Firewatchers & Women's Rest Room			
48	Boiler House & Dope Shop			
49	Air Compressor Shed			
50	Blister Hangar Main Stores			
51	Barrack Stores			
52	Latrines			
53	Staff Rest Room			
54	Civilian Canteen			
55	Sick Quarters			
56	Parachute Training Machine			
57	Pilots Locker & Rest Room			

A training/lecture block (65), Link Trainer building (63), library (64) and attendant ablutions were built near to the western edge of Henry Wood, the corner of trees being removed for visibility. The library block has long gone but East Herts Flying Club/North London Aero Club now occupy part of the lecture block as a clubroom. A great deal of clearing of the site was undertaken from 1993 to 1994 to demolish and remove unsafe structures and create a more accessible site for aircraft parking. The Station HQ (59 and 60) stood nearby and was demolished in 1993 as vandalism had made it unsafe. The station sick quarters (55), a 70ft x 20ft wooden hut opened in 1944, is now long gone. The canteen (54) was civilian run with a rest room (53) close by. Handcraft huts (51) and (57) were used as barrack stores and pilots' locker and rest room respectively and constructed of moulded asbestos. These were in frequent use until 1992 and after being vandalised suffered demolition in the summer of 1993. The Panshanger School of Flying used a third Handcraft hut (58) until 1992 and this, ironically, had always been the instructors' rest and locker room. A parachute-training machine (56) has long gone though the hardstanding still exists. A large materials store (50) was a 45ft-wide blister hangar, used as such until burned down in the 1980s. Building 48 was the boiler house and dope shop situated next to a Jane's corrugated hut (47) used as a women's rest room. The two Miskin Extra-Over blister hangars, 46 and 41, face each other still, with 46 containing a small annex workshop for engine maintenance and demonstration. The original canvas covers fitted for weather protection have disintegrated but anchor rings for them exist still in the concrete hardstanding. 41 was modified with corrugated frontage and large metal sliding doors but these have been removed a long time ago. A high earth bank isolates these hangars from the access road. This is out-fill from Panshanger Park and was deposited during 1995.

The main entrance to the airfield by 1943 became via Panshanger Lane, the B1000–A414 link road and you still enter the site this way passing the remains of two guards' huts on one's right. The guards prided their patch of ground and the whitewashed stones lining the path can still be found in the undergrowth. Both the guards' hut and sleeping quarters (Handcraft buildings) were destroyed in the early 1990s.

There have been a few changes to buildings since the Air Ministry map was drawn up. The coke compound (39) and blister hangar (38) were present until the late 1950s but certainly the compound removed to make way for a more modern brick-ended hangar. This has corrugated-iron sides and appears to have used corrugated roofing from another building, possibly 75 from the north site. The hangar had large sliding doors, facing west but these have long gone and it is now in a parlous state having been damaged by gales and vandals. A high earth bank (out-fill from the gravel extraction going on in Panshanger Park) is the primary reason it still stands.

Blister hangar 38 was still standing in the late 1980s but soon vandalised and destroyed by early 1992. A 'new' flight hut (Laing type) was erected to the north of this hangar during 1945 and lasted until the late 1980s.

There was a period of modernisation from 1958 until 1960, culminating in the completion of the T2 hangar. In addition a long, narrow, brick-walled hangar was completed in 1959. This has a pitched roof, faces east–west with sliding doors at either end and was built a few yards north of building 48. In 1962 this housed the newly imported Rallye aircraft.

The T2 dominates the scene on the south side however and was erected during 1960, placed to the west of the Station HQ. It seems to have been purchased new since they were still available and highly adaptable structures. A large concrete hardstanding was completed for access from the eastern end only and no one can recall the western-facing doors being used. Unconventionally it is a narrow-width T2 (95ft) and was confused for a while as a T1 but it is 239ft 7in in length with twenty-three bays and some 25ft in height, making it a hybrid T2. The reason for the purchase of the T2 was to expand Panshanger's business operations and Airwork Services used the hangar for final erection and sales of Cessna aircraft. After its heyday, through use by Lotus Cars, private fliers, a film studio for the Milk Marketing Board and Autair helicopters, the T2 today is a rusting hulk and no longer used for hangarage of aircraft.

Initially there were two windsocks (sleeve streamers) for the airfield, one near to the lecture blocks and one on the south-west boundary, beyond the decoy site. These were removed (post-1952) and replaced by one on the west boundary (near the footpath) with another in the

The south site lecture block is shown here, largely still intact and close to the current North London Aero Club facility. (Author)

far north-east corner. By the late 1980s the encroachment of housing and vandalism caused all to be removed and now the East Herts Flying Club uses a single windsock placed just north of the old signals square.

In 1994 East Herts Flying Club erected a small canvas-covered hangar to house the Pitts Special (G-HISS) and David Forshaw's Tipsy Trainer, G-AFSC. Later a similar-style hangar was erected adjacent to the T2 entrance to enable aircraft servicing to continue through the year. Currently this houses the construction of a Vans RV-6 light aircraft for the aerodrome manager.

In 2005 another prefabricated hangar was erected to the eastern edge of the parking stands and this houses the interesting Ultimate Kits Spitfire Mk.26, owned by John Pearson. This hanger has been joined recently by two more and changes have been made to the maintenance hangarage by the club house (2006).

The brick-walled hangar was built on the south site in the late 1950s and believed to be for the construction of the Somers Kendall SK.1 jet-powered racing aircraft. In the event the sole SK.1 was built at Woodley, Berkshire. The hangar is long and narrow and housed a procession of small aircraft only. (Author)

The two handcraft huts at the south entrance to the aerodrome have long gone but this 1993 view shows the main guard hut. Handcraft hutting was built by Universal Asbestos Ltd and made, as the name suggests, of asbestos concrete moulded into sections to form a 35'9" x 18' hut without an inner frame. Even in 1993 the pathway to the hut still contained white-washed stones. (Author)

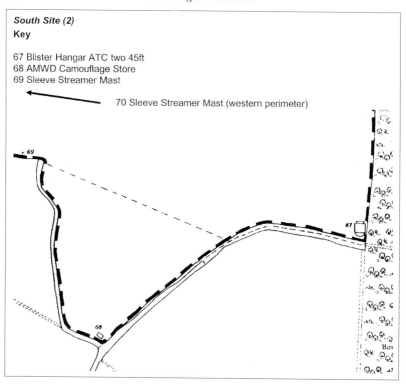

South Site (2)

Key
67 Blister Hangar ATC two 45ft
68 AMWD Camouflage Store
69 Sleeve Streamer Mast
Crown Copyright, RAF Museum.
Crown Copyright material is reproduced with the permission of the Controller of Her Majesty's Stationery Office.

This area was the site for the decoy factory and is now Moneyhole Lane Park.

The Air Training Corps hangar was used for glider storage. Suffice it to say nothing exists of the buildings here since the land was landscaped in the 1980s. The wood to the right is Birchall Wood. This extends into Henry Wood to the north.

There are two military installations that escaped being added to the plan, both airfield defence items. Two Allan Williams steel turrets were found on the airfield boundary, one on the western edge and the other guarding the north overlooking the Mimram Valley. As mentioned in the text the Long Ley turret was dug up during excavations for the self-build houses in the early 1980s and the cupola presented to the Panshanger School of Flying. Of the northern turret nothing more is known.

APPENDIX 3A

Taken from the Works Area Drawing PR 187 of 1944, with amendments of 1952 (WA Dwg PR 192).

Building Detail

SHEDULE OF BUILDINGS – PANSHANGER AIRFIELD 1944 & 1952★

Building No.	Building	Construction
1	Guard House	Brick
2	Link Trainer Store	Nissen Hutting
3	Link Trainer	Brick
4	Petrol Installation Aviation 4000 gal ex US	Brick
5	Latrines six Elsans, three UB	Brick
6	Coke Compound	Brick
7	Gas Defence Centre 60ft x 18ft	Laing Hutting
8	M.T. Storage 45ft Blister Hangar	Miskin
9	L Flight Hut	Thorn Hutting
10	B Flight Store	Brick
11	B Flight Locker Room 25ft x 16ft	Janes Corrugated Hutting
12	Fire Pool Hut	Brick
13	Dope Store	Brick
14	Latrines (Part Disused) two UB Bucket	Brick
15	B Flight Hut	Laing Hutting
16	M.T. Shed	Brick
17	Clothing Store 54ft x 10ft	Whitlock Hutting
18	R.A.F. Mess	Laing Hutting
19	Drying Room & Latrine two W.C. one U	Brick
20	Baths & Ablutions Block	Brick
21	Latrines	Brick
22	Destructor Horsfall Type	Brick
23	Armoury	Brick
24	Coke Compound	
25	Barrack Hut 60ft x 18ft for six	Laing Hutting
26	Barrack Hut 60ft x 18ft for ten	Laing Hutting
27	Ration Store 50ft x 20ft	Wood
28	N.F.E. Store 36ft x 16ft	Nissen Hutting
29	A.M.W.D. Store 36ft x 16ft	Nissen Hutting
30	Station Contractors Store 33ft x 10ft	Wood GCI
31	Sewage Disposal Works	
32	Blister Hangar B Flight 60ft	Miskin
33	Lubricating Oil Tanks two 500 gallon	
34	Petrol Installation Aviation two 12000 gal ex US	
35	Petrol Installation M.T. two 500 gal ex US	
36	Compass Base	Concrete
37	Ammunition Store	Brick
38	Blister Hangar three x 45ft combined	Miskin
39	Coke Compound	
40	Lubricant & Inflammable Store	Nissen Hutting
41	Blister Hangar Storage two 69 ft	Miskin

42	Guard Sleeping Quarters 36ft x 18ft one LB	Handcraft Hutting
43	Main Guard Hut 36ft x 18ft one WC one LB	Handcraft Hutting
44	Fire Pool Hut	Brick
45	Static Water 30,000 gallon	
46	Blister Hangar & Annex Maintenance two 69ft	Miskin
47	Firewatchers & Women's Rest Room	Janes Corrugated Hutting
48	Boiler House & Dope Store	
49	Air Compressor Shed	Janes Corrugated Hutting
50	Blister Hangar Main Stores two 45ft	Miskin
51	Barrack Stores	Handcraft Hutting
52	Latrines five WC six U	Brick
53	Staff Rest Room 30ft x 15ft	Wood
54		Wood & Janes
	Civilian Canteen	Corrugated
55	Sick Quarters 70ft x 20ft	Wood
56	Parachute Training Machine	Concrete
57	Pilots Locker & Rest Room 36ft x 16ft	Handcraft Hutting
58	Instructors Locker & Rest Room	Handcraft Hutting
59	Station Headquarters & Watch Tower five WC four U five LB	SECO
60	Switch House	Brick
61	Sub Station	Brick
62	Latrines five WC six U	Brick
63	Link Trainer	Brick
64	Library	Brick
65	Lecture Block	Brick
66	Sleeve Streamer Mast	Wood
67	Blister Hangar A.T.C. Hangar two 45ft	Miskin
68	A.M.W.D. Camouflage Store	Brick
69	Sleeve Streamer Mast	Wood
70	Sleeve Streamer Mast	Wood
71	Grenade & S.A.A. Store	Brick
72	Blister Hangar B Flight	Miskin
73	Incendiary Bomb & Component Store 15ft x 10ft	Wood & GCI
74	Blister Hangar L Flight 45ft	Miskin
75	Blister Hangar L Flight 60ft	Miskin
76	Barrack Hut for ten★	SECO
77	Barrack Hut for ten★	SECO
78	Barrack Hut for ten★	SECO

★ By 1952 someone seems to have forgotten a Laing hut to the north of blister hangar 38 on the south site. This does not appear in the amended plan and was evident from late 1945/early 1946. It was probably a 'new' building from surplus.

Hangars

Blisters

The blister hangar was designed by consulting engineers Norman & Dawbarn and William C. Inman of C.H. Miskin & Sons, a local engineering company. The blister was a small arched shed for storage of aircraft, maintenance of same or motor transport. Around the UK there were three main sizes (plus variations) but Panshanger appears to have only two sizes, the standard wooden blister of 45ft span, 25ft length and 14ft height and the Extra-Over, a welded steel lattice structure of 69ft span, 45ft length and 20ft 4in height. The standard blister was built in arched wooden sections some 5ft apart, bolted together. The arch was supported on wooden bearers and restrained by vertical posts. At the side wall wooden decking was laid over the bearers and the structure normally covered with corrugated iron. There was no need for a foundation with the structure simply anchored with irons staked into the ground. The floor was usually left to earth with tools or stores placed on the decking. The hangar ends had quick-release canvas curtains that formed a conical tent adding to the floor space secured to steel rings embedded into the earth. The larger steel blister was an all-welded series of ribs bolted together 7ft 6in apart using steel ties and purlins of steel or wood. Although originally laid on earth the steel blisters were floored with concrete later to provide a better surface for larger aircraft types.

'T2' Hangar

See earlier

Huts

At the time the airfield and the buildings were constructed, from mid-1941 until late 1943 there was an acute shortage of adequate raw material for hutting. Strategic materials (steel and wood) were in short supply and expensive and alternative construction methods being pioneered. These are noted in the use of asbestos, plasterboard and corrugated-iron hutting, which provided a cost-effective and simple solution to demand if barely satisfying the requirements. That said, despite the proposed short lifespan of these buildings it was only in the early 1990s that the last Handcraft hut ceased to be occupied. Even today (2006) several Seco and a Nissen can still be seen.

GCI

There was one example erected of this wooden hut, a 33ft x 10ft building on the north site for the aerodrome contractors (30).

Handcraft

From May 1942 the Universal Asbestos Co. Ltd manufactured these huts at Handcraft Works, Tolpits Lane, Watford. They consisted of asbestos cement sections with seven flats, inverted to form a trough and bolted together. There was no frame, with the internal walls lined with asbestos sheet. Cement-rendered brick was used for each end. Dimensions were 35ft 9in long, 18ft span and 9ft high in the centre.

Janes

A refined version of the Laing hut, where plasterboard was replaced by corrugated iron. It is thought that Boulton & Paul built Jane huts. All on the south side have been demolished.

Laing

Plasterboard huts, originally made in Elstree by John Laing, consisted of a wooden frame clad internally and externally with plasterboard. To prevent the weather getting in, the external plaster was covered in felt sheeting. These buildings were usually delivered in prefabricated kits to order. It appears that a Laing hut was erected on the south site in 1945, positioned next to blister hangar 38. This was the flight hut for the RFS and later the London Aeroplane Club and is evident in the aerial photograph of 1945.

Nissen

This highly successful hut was designed in 1915 by Canadian Colonel P.N. Nissen. A UK factory was set up at Rye House, Hoddesdon in 1922 and continued to produce the huts until 1960 after Schreiber Wood Industries had taken over the company two years earlier. All Nissens were 16ft-diameter semicircular section with corrugated-iron sheets bolted onto 'T' section steel ribs 6ft apart with bracing wires to hold all together. Inevitably various multiples of 6ft lengths were possible. The ends usually containing two windows and a doorframe were timber framed, clad with wooden boarding and felt. For more strength brick ends could be used. One Nissen on the north site remains.

Seco

These were mixed plywood and asbestos huts designed by Uni-Seco in 1942 and sub-contracted to various construction companies, the most successful being En-Tout-Cas at Thurmaston, Leicester. Extensive use of plywood was made, forming hollow prefabricated beams, columns and eaves. A timber frame was fitted to a wooden keel, in turn fixed to a concrete base. Flat asbestos sheet was fixed to a timber frame and the cavity filled with cement and wood wool with the unit profiled to fit the main frame. Flat-pack kits were delivered to the Ministry of Works Central Storage Depot at Elstow, near Bedford and distributed to RAF sites. At Panshanger Seco huts housed the airmen and were added to the north site from 1951. These remain occupied to the current day. On the south site Seco provided the aerodrome headquarter building.

Whitlock

This was a similar building to the Laing, measuring 54ft long and 10ft wide. Only one was erected at Panshanger, used as a clothing store. This is timber framed, clad in cedar wood with a felted wood roof.

APPENDIX 4

The Films

Panshanger has been used for the backdrop and as part of the plot in a few films. In 1948 a 16mm silent black and white film was made of the AOC visit, giving a rare view of the RFS Tiger Moths. More recently Panshanger School of Flying initiated a series of Flying Training videos and at least one advertisement for a national bank, all made at Panshanger. There are no doubt many other home movies and videos shot at the airfield and, hopefully, these will emerge with time.

Operation Bullshine

During December 1958 and January 1959 the airfield was used for the making of a wartime comedy film *Operation Bullshine*, starring Barbara Murray and Donald Sinden. Masquerading as a Luftwaffe aircraft for the film at Panshanger was Airspeed Oxford, G-AHGU.

Follow that Horse

The film crews moved in again during 1960 for the making of *Follow that Horse*, starring David Tomlinson, using the Control Tower as a backdrop for some scenes.

The Devil Rides Out

A scene involving the veteran Moth, G-EBLV, was shot at Panshanger on 3 October 1967. Two fifteen-minute sessions were edited down to four seconds in the film!

The Bofors Gun

In 1968 the *Bofors Gun* was shot at Panshanger and starred Jack Gold, Nicole Williamson, Ian Holm and David Warner.

The Battle of Britain

There is conflicting evidence that scenes from the 1969 United Artists epic were shot at Panshanger. When the film was being made aerial sequences were shot over the airfield and the Sir Frederic Osborn School, using aircraft from the main base at Duxford, and it is highly likely the aerodrome served a useful purpose in refuelling and rest stops. No sequence involving the aerodrome has been used in the film.

Rentadick

Made in 1971 and 1972 and starring all manner of the cream of British comedy actors, climaxed at Panshanger. Some of the buildings, including the T2 hangar, already looking worse for wear, were used as the backdrop for the final scene whereupon a Bristol Superfreighter, G-APAV, on loan from Midland Air Cargo, takes off into the sunset. The Superfreighter was a spectacular sight as it cleared the Sir Frederic Osborn School, near the threshold of the east-west runway, with some ease.

Our Miss Fred

A film starring Danny La Rue was made during 1972 and the airfield and buildings became a German airfield for the duration. A replica Spanish-built Messerschmitt Bf109 adorned the grass for the period and a de Havilland Dragon Rapide was based for the period, painted in German markings.

The Muppet Movie

The Muppet Movie was made during 1979 and 1980 and involved a Douglas Dakota with scenes being shot on the airfield. Other films, one starring Peter Sellers and another with Walther Matthau, have been noted and, as noted earlier, numerous television adverts have used the airfield and hangars as backdrops.

TV Series

Scenes from an episode of the late 1960s TV series *The Champions* (Associated British) were filmed using the control building as a backdrop. A de Havilland Dove was used for a few scenes.

An episode of the BBC TV comedy *Fairly Secret Army*, starring Geoffrey Palmer, was shot at Panshanger in 1984.

Advertisements

In 1970 the Milk Marketing Board used a 20ft-high, prefabricated milk bottle for an advertisement utilising the T2 hangar.

During the 1980s Panshanger School of Flying used a Piper Tomahawk as part of an advert for a national bank.

Any further information about the use of the aerodrome for films and TV would be greatly appreciated.

APPENDIX 5

Panshanger Estate Sale: Areas of Land Concerning the Airfield 15 July 1953.

Panshanger estate was key to the airfield's existence and the closure of the house following the lack of a natural heir brought about the sale. The last heir was William Henry Grenfell, Baron Desborough, who resided at Taplow Court, Buckinghamshire. He had married Ethel Anne Priscilla Fane on 17 February 1887, who survived him. She inherited Panshanger House and the Cowper Estates on the death of Countess Cowper in 1913. She did not elect to live at Panshanger due to the house acquiring crippling maintenance costs and as a result it was left to decay. She died on 28 May 1952, survived by two daughters, Monica (Lady Salmond) and Alexandra (Viscountess Gage) and the estate went to auction.

The auction of Panshanger House, substantial land (3,224 acres) and buildings took place at Hertford Corn Exchange, 11.00 a.m. on 15 July 1953. Messrs Humbert & Flint were the auctioneers. Lots as listed below involved all land requisitioned by the Air Ministry in 1940.

Lot	Description	Acres	Rent (per annum)
Two	Warrengate and Marden Farm	484.328	£745 10s (£745.50)
Five	Tewinbury Farm	353.700	£526 1s (£526.07½)
Six	Attimore Hall Farm	293.564	£376 8s (£376.40)
Twelve	Woodlands nr Cole Green	169.335 (157.475 vacant acres)	

Description:

Lot Two: Warrengate and Marden Dairy Farm
A 'well equipped dairy farm at present supporting a producer retailer milk business and let to Mr C J Barton at a yearly rental of £745 10s 0d (£745.50), last adjusted 29 September 1951. Included are 169.676 acres lying to the south of the Hertford to Welwyn road under requisition by the Air Ministry direct from the tenant at a requisition rental of £158 3s 0d per annum (£158.15)'.

NB: Mr C.J. Barton acquired 8.671 acres of land (part of Plot 252) just north of the RAF Mess prior to the auction and therefore the 1953 figure is smaller than the original amount requisitioned by the Air Ministry.

The entire Lot was withdrawn from further bidding at £23,000.

Lot Five: Tewinbury Farm, Tewin
'A large farm of 353 acres three rood and thirteen perches let to Mr T Williams at an annual rent of £526 1s 6d (£526.7½p). Included are 11.75 acres of plot OS310 (Tewin Parish) under requisition by the Air Ministry direct for the tenant at £13 12s 0d' (£13.60). This land was on the western edge of the airfield, bordering the north-south bridleway.

In addition to the land the purchaser was obliged to include the de Havilland 'Outer Marker' beacon which had been added in May 1953 at an annual rent of £2. After purchase of the land by Nat Somers the beacon was serviced until the late 1960s when a brick building erected in Archers Green replaced it.

Lot Six: Attimore Hall Farm
Farmed by the tenant, Mr John S. Crawford. The land under requisition by the Air Ministry direct from the vendor amounted to 36.007 acres in Hertingfordbury Parish and 10.347 in Tewin Parish, some 46.354 acres in all.

All of this land had been used for the decoy factory, in the 'V' formed by Moneyhole Lane and Green Lane/Birchall & Henry Wood.

This land was sold to Mr Crawford for £12,500

Lot Twelve: Woodlands near Cole Green

Henry Wood measured 26.609 acres with 11.860 (plot 261) under requisition by the Air Ministry from the vendor at a rental of £4 15s per annum (£4.75).

The top left-hand corner of Henry Wood was 'landscaped' (trees removed) in 1942 to provide better siting for the runways.

Excluding roads (Green Lane, Moneyhole Lane and other tracks) the land encompassed by the airfield in 1941 was 229.905 acres. With further acquisition in 1943 from Marden Dairy Farm to construct the south site this grew to 247.83 acres.

APPENDIX 6

Entrants in the London to Cardiff Air Race, 2 June 1961:

G-APZZ/2	Druine D.31 Turbulent
G-ARIZ/3	Rollason Druine D.31 Turbulent
G-APIZ/4	Rollason Druine D.31 Turbulent
G-AHGZ/5	Taylorcraft Plus D
G-APNZ/7	Rollason Druine D.31 Turbulent
G-APMZ/12	Rollason Druine D.31 Turbulent
G-AOAA/14	De Havilland DH.82A Tiger Moth
G-ANMZ/15	De Havilland DH.82A Tiger Moth
G-AOUY/16	De Havilland DH.82A Tiger Moth
G-AREH/17	De Havilland DH.82A Tiger Moth
G-ARAZ/18	De Havilland DH.82A Tiger Moth
G-AOTM/19	De Havilland DHC-1 Chipmunk 22A
G-ANZU/20	De Havilland DH.82A Tiger Moth
G-ACDC/21	De Havilland DH.82A Tiger Moth
G-ANZZ/22	De Havilland DH.82A Tiger Moth
G-ARHA/25	Forney F.1A Aircoupe
G-APRA/28	De Havilland DH.82A Tiger Moth
G-ANEI/30	De Havilland DH.82A Tiger Moth
G-AHKY/35	Miles M.18 Srs.2
G-ABUS/41	Comper CLA.7 Swift
G-AIUA/43	Miles M.14A Hawk Trainer III
G-ABVE/48	Arrow Active II
G-APAM/52	De Havilland DH.82A Tiger Moth
G-AIUE/57	Miles M.14A Hawk Trainer III
G-AOEJ/63	Percival P.34 Proctor 3
G-AHFK/64	Percival P.34 Proctor 3
G-ALFX/68	Percival P.34 Proctor 3
G-AIHD/72	Percival P.34 Proctor 3
G-ALZG/80	Miles M.65 Gemini 3C
G-ANZJ/88	Percival P.31 Proctor 4
G-ARAT/90	Cessna 180C
G-APZS/91	Cessna 175A Skylark
G-ADTD/94	Miles M.3D Falcon Six
G-ADGP/96	Miles M.2L Hawk Speed Six
G-AIDN/99	Vickers Supermarine 502 Spitfire Tr.8 (eventual winner)
OO-ARE/100	Vickers Supermarine 361 Spitfire LF.IXe (retired at Exeter)

Sources and Acknowledgements

Barry Abraham, Geoff Archer, A.R. 'Pop' Bilkey, Alan Brackley, David Bray, Darryl Cott, Gerry Cullen, Paul Doyle, Maurice Freeman, Ken Green, John Hunt, David Jones, Gordon Leeke, Graham Lewis, Jim Mead, Malcolm Moulding, David Oliver, Arthur W.J.G. Ord-Hume, Grant Peerless, Martin Pole, Terry Pole, Richard Riding, Geoffrey Robinson, Stuart Spicer, Ralph Steiner, Nick Stroud, Ian Thirsk, Andrew Warren, Doug Watson, Bob Wolfenden, Mike Yalden.
795 Squadron (Harpenden) and 1166 Squadron (Welwyn Garden City) Air Training Corps
Air Britain - Ken Border, Malcolm Fillmore, Bill Fisher, AB-IX
Association of Transport Photographers – Bob Jenner-Hobbs,
Aviation Photo News
BAE SYSTEMS – Mike Fielding/Barry Guess
De Havilland Aircraft Museum Trust, London Colney
East Herts Flying School/North London Flying School/Haim Merkado
Hertfordshire Archives & Local Studies, Hertford
Military Aviation Photographs – Brian Pickering
National Archives, Kew
RAF Museum Hendon – Dept of Research & Information Services
Welwyn Garden City Library
Welwyn Hatfield Times

Bibliography

Austen, Michael, *British Civil Aircraft Registers* 1919 – 1999, Air Britain 1999

Barrymore-Halpenny, Bruce, *Action Stations 8*, 1984

Chapman, John, and Goodall, Geoff, *Warbirds Directory*, 1996

Dobinson, Colin, *Fields of Deception*, 2000

Francis, Paul, *British Military Airfield Architecture*, 1996

Jackson, A.J., *British Civil Aircraft Volumes 1, 2 & 3*, 1974

Jackson, A.J., *De Havilland Aircraft Since 1909*, 1978

Lewis, Peter, *British Racing & Record-Breaking Aircraft*, 1970

Read, Robin, *Colin Chapman's Lotus*

Merton-Jones, Tony, *British Independent Airlines Since 1946*

Ord-Hume, Arthur W.J.G., *Flight on Frail Wings, On Home Made Wings*

Sturtivant ISO, Ray; Hamlin, John & Halley MBE, James J, *Royal Air Force Flying Training & Support Units*

Aeroplane, Aeroplane Monthly
Air Pictorial
Air Reserve Gazette
Aviation News
De Havilland Gazette
De Havilland Moth Club Enterprise Magazine
Flight International
Flypast Magazine
LAAS International
The Aeroplane Directory of British Aviation 1963 Edition
Welwyn Hatfield Times

Index

If you are interested in purchasing other books published by Tempus, or in case you have difficulty finding any Tempus books in your local bookshop, you can also place orders directly through our website.

www.tempus-publishing.com